101
GINS
TO TRY BEFORE YOU DIE

IAN BUXTON

BIRLINN

First published in Great Britain in 2015
by Polygon, an imprint of Birlinn Ltd
West Newington House
10 Newington Road
Edinburgh
EH9 1QS

www.birlinn.co.uk

ISBN: 978 1 78027 299 3
Copyright © Ian Buxton, 2015

British Library Cataloguing-in-Publication Data
A catalogue record for this book is available on request from the British Library

Designed by Teresa Monachino
Printed and bound by 1010 Printing International, China

CONTENTS

INTRODUCTION

We're in the middle of a new Gin Craze. From being the drink of choice of middle-aged, Jaguar-driving golfers and an easy target for stand-up comedians, today it's harder to find anything hipper on the international bar scene.

This is by way of an exploration. I want to see how Madam Geneva, scourge of the drinking classes and emblematic of wantonness, sin and ruin has evolved into the most fashionable of spirits. How a drink reeking of suburbia, Home Counties complacency and golf-club lounges is now found in cutting-edge cocktail bars around the world. And how what you might once have described as the Nigel Farage of drinks has morphed into its Cara Delevingne. (*Disclaimer:* I have no idea what the divine Cara drinks. We move in different circles, and for all I know she's tucked up in bed well before *News at Ten* with a tasty glass of organic green tea – the point, as I'm sure you've gathered, is that gin is *hot.*)[1]

Rowlandson and, famously, Hogarth placed gin at the heart of much of their work. Commentators too, such as Defoe, Fielding, Dickens and many others had much to say about it, not to mention those eighteenth-century politicians who legislated with such enthusiasm (and such a lack of noticeable effect) to curb the English taste for gin.

Or should that be Dutch? They gave the world 'genever' which the English made their own, leading rapidly to London's original (and infamous) Gin Craze. It may have taken more than 250 years, but gin has now shaken off its reputation for debauchery and ruin to take its place as one of the hottest of world spirits.

So, from Adnams to Xoriguer (couldn't find a Z I liked; you'll see) and London to Plymouth (and beyond) I want to explore this incredible explosion of innovative gin brands and the new generation of young and enthusiastic distillers that are reinventing this most English of drinks.

Not that a hint of debauchery and ruin does its image any harm. But today it's all very confusing. Scarcely a day goes by without an

---

1. Though conventionally served ice cold, of course.

established brand offering a fresh take on their established styles or, more likely, a new boutique distillery opening its doors – where gin is *de rigueur*. However, before we dive into that particular madness a little bit of history is probably called for.

A LITTLE BIT OF HISTORY

According to the Middlesex Magistrates, gin was 'the principal cause of all the vice and debauchery committed among the inferior sort of people'. Clearly those gentlemen took a robust and not very politically correct view of those making an involuntary and no doubt unwelcome visit to their court back in 1721 …

So things were pretty over-excited in Georgian England, which for most of the early eighteenth century was in the grip of a binge-drinking frenzy we've come to know as the Gin Craze. Daniel Defoe put up a pretty robust defence of the industry though:

> As to the excesses and intemperances of the People, and their drinking immoderate Quantities of Malt Spirits, the Distillers are not concern'd in it at all; their Business is to prepare a Spirit wholesome and good. If the People will destroy themselves by their own Excesses, and make that Poison, which is otherwise an Antidote; 'tis the Magistrates' Business to help that, not the Distillers. (*The Case of the Distillers,* London, 1726)

Mind you, he'd been well paid for that piece of enthusiastic spin-doctoring and was as liable to take the side of the moral majority as defend the distilling industry which, incidentally and apart from some pious sermonising about 'using our products responsibly', hasn't to this day got much further than 'don't blame us if people get off their face on our products'.

You could quite reasonably argue that alcopops and cheap cider are today's equivalent of gin, though as far as I know, no one is yet selling these one shot at a time through a 'Puss and Mew' vending machine. Give them time, though, give them time.

Gin's history begins … well, no one can quite agree. According to some commentators, not least the ever reliable Wikipedia (so it must be true), the Dutch physician Franciscus Sylvius is to be credited with the invention of gin in the mid-seventeenth century.

But 'Dutch Courage' can be dated to 1585 when English troops supported the Dutch army in their war with the Spanish, and there are written references to 'genever' as early as the thirteenth century.

I'm not convinced that it matters. Various nations make various claims for the ancient origins of their national drink; the Scots date whisky to 1494, the Poles claim 1174 for vodka, and the French place Armagnac ahead of cognac with references to 1411. So the English were late to the game with gin, probably sometime in the early seventeenth century. The Worshipful Company of Distillers, Defoe's patron, received its royal warrant in 1638, but the first 'distillers' were actually surgeons, much to the displeasure of the apothecaries who took exception to these upstarts and objected to the dilution of their jealously guarded privileges.

The first attempts at gin were an effort to replicate the genever enjoyed by English troops during their long campaigns in Holland during the Thirty Years' War (1618–1648), but it took the arrival of King William III, or William of Orange as he is better known, in the Glorious Revolution of 1688 for gin to raise its game. And raise it, it did, in response to a series of laws aiming to promote distilling in England (and, not entirely coincidentally, the sale of grain – which suited the landed interest then dominant in Parliament very nicely indeed).

Soon sales of gin exceeded that of the more expensive beer; little wonder when anyone could start distilling by giving ten days' public notice. To the alarm of the genteel and the ruling classes production soared, and in 1729 a licensing system for distillers and publicans was introduced and duty charged. Things got worse: illicitly distilled 'gin' prospered at the expense of legitimate traders. Soon it was estimated that in certain parts of London one private house in four was selling some form of spirits. Regionally the situation was little better and an epidemic of alcohol dependency was taking hold of the poorer parts of the nation.

A further attempt at legislation, the Gin Act of September 1736, merely exacerbated the situation by attempting to restrict retailers and greatly raise the retail price. Though opposed by, among others, the Prime Minister (Sir Robert Walpole) and Dr Samuel Johnson, the law was passed – and then routinely ignored. Only two of the infamous £50 distilling licences (equivalent to around £750,000 today) were taken out, while production is thought to have increased by around half.

Rioting followed the passing of the Act, though street riots by the mob were not infrequent during this period: 1736 saw the Porteous Riots of April and September in Edinburgh, and in east London in July of that year there were riots against the cheap labour of Irish immigrants. A number of pamphlets arguing for and against the measure were issued, some with extravagant titles such as 'An Elegy on the much lamented death of the most excellent, the most truly beloved, and universally admired Lady Madam Geneva'. The lady also appeared in a famous print, 'The Funeral Procession of Madam Geneva'.

Social problems associated with excessive drinking and the public consumption of spirits, such as crime and prostitution, continued, and Parliament, accepting that the 1736 Act was unworkable, returned to the subject in 1742/43. The earlier legislation was abolished and a fairer system of licensing and taxation was introduced, partly following lobbying from the distilling industry. This was further refined in 1747, but the problems remained.

By 1751, the novelist and magistrate Henry Fielding, active in the suppression of the gin trade, attributed to it 'the late (i.e. recent) increase in robbers' and may have worked with or influenced his friend William Hogarth whose pair of engravings 'Gin Lane' and 'Beer Street' dramatically illustrate the scourge of excessive gin drinking in graphic scenes of misery, vice, degradation and death. Hogarth contrasts the squalor resulting from gin consumption with the robust health of the beer drinker, illustrating a street scene where only the pawnbroker's business appears to be suffering. Moralistic verses by the Revd James Townley appear beneath both images; his poem on gin beginning:

Gin, cursed Fiend, with Fury fraught,
Makes human Race a Prey.
It enters by a deadly Draught
And steals our Life away.

But by 1757 the Gin Craze had subsided. In part this was due to the 1751 legislation which required licensees to trade from premises rented for at least £10 a year and thus tended to favour larger, better-quality producers. Historians also point to population growth, poor harvests and the consequent reduction in wages and higher food prices as contributory factors. Gin production simply became less profitable, and so the trade declined until the next boom in Victorian times with the arrival of the Gin Palace.

These lavish and alluring premises flourished from the late 1820s and provided a vivid contrast to the squalid dram shops that preceded them. Large, dramatically lit and filled with cut-glass and mirrors, they were originally designed for fast service, where the patron was intended to consume his or her drink standing up and then leave to make way for the next customer. Their influence on pub design was profound and they made a notable impact on the novelist Charles Dickens who describes them at length in the *Evening Chronicle* of 19 February 1835:

All is light and brilliancy. The hum of many voices issues from that splendid gin-shop which forms the commencement of the two streets opposite; and the gay building with the fantastically ornamented parapet, the illuminated clock, the plate-glass windows surrounded by stucco rosettes, and its profusion of gas-lights in richly gilt burners, is perfectly dazzling when contrasted with the darkness and dirt we have just left. The interior is even gayer than the exterior. A bar of French-polished mahogany, elegantly carved, extends the whole width of the place; and there are two side-aisles of great casks, painted green and gold, enclosed within a light brass rail, and bearing such inscriptions, as 'Old Tom, 549'; 'Young Tom, 360'; 'Samson, 1421' – the figures agreeing, we presume, with 'gallons', understood. Beyond the bar is a lofty and spacious saloon, full of the same enticing vessels, with a gallery running round it, equally well furnished. On the counter, in addition to the usual spirit apparatus, are two or three little baskets of cakes and biscuits, which are carefully secured at top with wicker-work, to prevent their contents being unlawfully abstracted. Behind it, are two showily dressed damsels with large necklaces, dispensing the spirits and 'compounds'. They are assisted by the ostensible proprietor of the concern, a stout, coarse fellow in a fur cap, put on very much on one side to give him a knowing air, and to display his sandy whiskers to the best advantage.

In his essay, Dickens is highly critical of the prevailing social conditions of the poorer working classes and the unemployed but very well aware of the appeal of the gin palace. He concludes:

> Gin-drinking is a great vice in England, but wretchedness and dirt are a greater; and until you improve the homes of the poor, or persuade a half-famished wretch not to seek relief in the temporary oblivion of his own misery, with the pittance which, divided among his family, would furnish a morsel of bread for each, gin-shops will increase in number and splendour.

Later, in *The Life and Adventures of Martin Chuzzlewit* (1844) we meet the sublime Sairey Gamp: 'The face of Mrs Gamp – the nose in particular – was somewhat red and swollen, and it was difficult to enjoy her society without becoming conscious of a smell of spirits.' It would be some time before gin threw off the stereotype so vividly called up by Dickens.

However, as British imperial power expanded, to become at its zenith the empire on which the sun never set, the medicinal use of quinine to prevent malaria became more widespread. French scientists had extracted quinine from the bark of the cinchona tree in 1817, but the taste was bitter and unpalatable. Soon though, British officers in India, no doubt imbued with patriotic fervour and keen to support domestic industry while helping their medicine go down, hit on the idea of combining it with soda water, sugar, lime and gin.

Thus, as early as 1825 we see the forerunner of the gin and tonic, and gin beginning to move upmarket. Bottles of sweetened quinine water soon appeared and carbonated tonic water was introduced towards the end of the nineteenth century. Meanwhile Johann Schweppe had founded his eponymous business in Vienna in 1783 (he moved to London nine years later). Regardless of the many new brands of tonic now available, some of them excellent, Schweppes must surely be regarded as the most famous name in tonic and is inextricably linked with gin.

Some of the greatest names in gin date from this period, or just earlier. Greenall's was founded in 1761, Gordon's in 1769, and Plymouth in 1793, but with the advent of Tanqueray (1830) and Beefeater (1860s, but building on a firm established some forty years earlier) branding and marketing came to the fore.

Having swept round the British Empire, gin enjoyed its next moment of fame and popularity during the cocktail boom of the Roaring Twenties. Again, it had successfully moved upmarket and was fashionable, acceptable in society and had crossed the Atlantic to conquer America. The advent of Prohibition would not appear to have significantly dented its appeal, with the 'bathtub gin' of legend (and all too often, fact) lending it a brittle glamour and racy charm. The lure of the speakeasy and the blandishments of the bootlegger are an uncomfortable echo of England's Gin Craze.

As late as 1942, Rick (Humphrey Bogart) describes his bar in *Casablanca* as a 'gin joint' – something clandestine, outside the law and carrying the fascination of forbidden fruit.

By the 1950s, however, it had shaken off this raffish clothing and become respectable: now it was something served in golf clubs to the middle-aged and middle-class. Long-established brands began to fail, and old favourites such as Lemon Gin, Orange Gin and Old Tom fell away one by one. Little wonder that within a few short years vodka and white rum would overtake it and gin's slow decline would accelerate. But, as we will see, that was to be reversed even more recently with the arrival of brands such as Bombay (and Bombay Sapphire) and Hendrick's.

Which brings us pretty much up to today, where we find an excitement and energy about gin that has not been seen for more than a hundred years. Today there are probably in excess of 500 brands available worldwide, with more arriving virtually daily.

Sadly, I haven't room for them all – but here are 101 to try before you die!

HOW GIN IS MADE

This is the briefest of descriptions because a number of books and many websites deal with the technical description in great depth and with considerable expertise. Many of the brand entries also expand on aspects of production.

Gin is made from high-strength pure distilled spirits, normally from grain or molasses, which is selected for its clean neutral flavour.

How Gin is made at the Edinburgh Gin Distillery

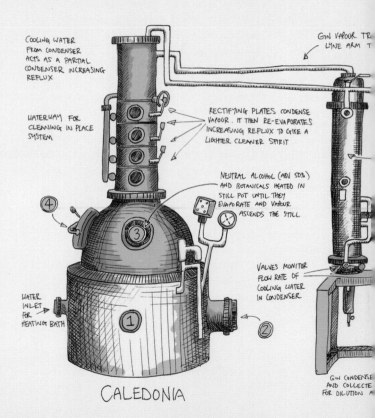

COOLING WATER
FROM CONDENSER
ACTS AS A PARTIAL
CONDENSER INCREASING
REFLUX

GIN VAPOUR TR
LYNE ARM T

WATERWAY FOR
CLEANING IN PLACE
SYSTEM

RECTIFYING PLATES CONDENSE
VAPOUR . IT THEN RE-EVAPORATES
INCREASING REFLUX TO GIVE A
LIGHTER CLEANER SPIRIT

NEUTRAL ALCOHOL (ABV 50%)
AND BOTANICALS HEATED IN
STILL POT UNTIL THEY
EVAPORATE AND VAPOUR
ASCENDS THE STILL

④

③

VALVES MONITOR
FLOW RATE OF
COOLING WATER
IN CONDENSER

WATER
INLET
FOR
HEATING BATH

①

②

GIN CONDENSE
AND COLLECTE
FOR DILUTION A

CALEDONIA

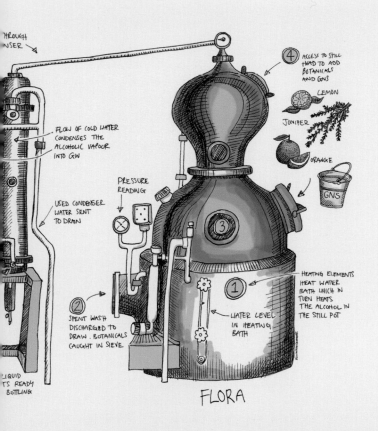

THROUGH
NSER

FLOW OF COLD WATER
CONDENSES THE
ALCOHOLIC VAPOUR
INTO GIN

USED CONDENSER
WATER SENT
TO DRAIN

PRESSURE
READING

② SPENT WASH
DISCHARGED TO
DRAIN. BOTANICALS
CAUGHT IN SIEVE

IQUID
TS READY
BOTTLING

④ ACCESS TO STILL
HEAD TO ADD
BOTANICALS
AND GNS

LEMON

JUNIPER

ORANGE

GNS

③

① HEATING ELEMENTS
HEAT WATER
BATH WHICH IN
TURN HEATS
THE ALCOHOL IN
THE STILL POT

WATER LEVEL
IN HEATING
BATH

FLORA

Grape-based spirit and, occasionally, beetroot may also be used, though neutral grain spirit (NGS) predominates. In the case of London Dry gin, the best-known style, the neutral spirit is redistilled in the presence of botanicals to give the resultant gin its flavour. Following distillation, nothing is permitted to be added other than neutral alcohol, water to reduce the spirit to bottling strength, and a tiny amount of sugar. 'London' defines the style, and production may take place anywhere: it does not indicate geographical origin

Starting with juniper, which must be its main or characteristic flavour, gin derives its nose and taste from botanicals, which are simply natural herbs and spices such as coriander, orange and lemon peel, cinnamon, nutmeg, angelica and cardamom. Orris root is frequently used in more expensive products, not only for its flavour but because it acts to integrate and bind other flavours together. Botanical recipes, which may be of considerable age, are unique to each brand. These recipes are often a closely guarded secret, though some distillers, commendably in my view, print the details on their bottles or labels. Traditionally, no more than ten or a dozen botanicals would have been used; today, some recipes call for as many as forty-seven different herbs and spices. In recent years there has been a trend for distillers to experiment with ever more exotic or rare botanicals in an effort to develop new flavours and make their product stand out from the crowd.

Distilled gin, often considered a lesser category, is made in a similar way to London gin, but it is permitted to add further flavourings, both natural and artificial, on completion of distillation.

The legal minimum alcohol level in the EU is 37.5% alcohol by volume (abv), although most standard and premium brands are bottled and sold at a higher strength. This, of course, affects the price, not least because duty is charged according to the alcoholic content of the finished product. As gin, unlike whisky or brandy, does not require any maturation it may be bottled immediately, though many brands elect to 'rest' the spirit for some days or weeks to allow all the flavours to integrate fully. There has also been a recent trend to age gin in wooden casks to add colour and further develop flavour.

A third method is 'cold compounding', in which the essential oils from the botanicals are either distilled or simply pressed out and then added to the spirit. The resulting product may be labelled as 'gin', but not 'distilled' or 'London' gin. While in the past this method would have been reserved for cheaper, lower-quality products there are today some more interesting and innovative expressions made in this way by smaller producers.

Brief mention should be made of the cold vacuum method, which often uses a piece of laboratory apparatus known as a rota-vap (rotary evaporator). By distilling under a vacuum, significantly lower temperatures may be used. It is argued that the more subtle and volatile elements of certain botanicals are thereby preserved and the resulting spirit is fresher and more vibrant in taste. A number of smaller producers are making gin in this way.

At the more experimental end of the market, producers are 'finishing' gins in casks previously used for a range of products such as malt whisky and even barrel-aged cocktails. An example is the Batshit Mental range of products, which includes a Negroni-Aged Bathtub Gin. However, such expressions are something of a minority taste, and while they add colour and great variety they account for only a tiny percentage of the global market. Only a few years ago they would have been unthinkable.

Last but not least, it is worth noting that the biggest gin market in the world is the Philippines, accounting for more than 40% of global sales. The local favourite, by a country mile, is Ginebra San Miguel, but, because it is rarely seen beyond its home territory, it doesn't make my 101.

101 GINS

No one really knows how many gin brands are available worldwide (there are probably well over 500), but a selection had to be made. Inevitably it's a personal choice, but I hope that you enjoy my collection and agree that it would make a splendid gin list or back bar.

In the interests of including as many producers as possible, I endeavoured not to list multiple styles of any one single brand, though some expressions seemed so very different or interesting that they were eventually admitted.

For some time I held a strong personal bias in favour of those brands that were actually produced by the principals. It seemed reasonable to prefer companies that made their own products over those that simply went to a contract distiller with a concept or recipe and had some gin made for them, especially as provenance seems likely to become increasingly important. However, I realised that this would not only rule out some very interesting and enjoyable products but that for some fledgling ventures this was their only route to market. Having established their brand, it was clear that some at least would then take the more capital-intensive route of becoming a distiller in their own right. There is more than one example of that in the listings.

While writing this book I quickly lost count of the number of producers, particularly small ones, who assured me of the 'passion' of their founders and wanted to tell me of their 'journey' and the 'hand-crafted' and 'artisanal' nature of their brand, evidently in the belief that this made them stand out in some way. It does not!

In the course of my 'journey' (how I have come to loathe that word) I visited many, many distilleries, some of them very, very large indeed. I did not see any robots making the gin, and master distillers such as Desmond Payne (Beefeater), Tom Nichol (Tanqueray), Nik Fordham (Bombay) and their colleagues in other equally large plants exhibited an enthusiasm, commitment and sheer excitement about their work that was the equal of any neophyte toiling over a forty-litre alembic in an old farm building or inner-city light-industrial unit. They may sell many, many times the volume of their up-and-coming competitors and they may not stick the labels on by hand but the quality of their products and the joy in making it that they freely shared with me should not be underestimated.

My not very original conclusion is that it is the taste that matters!

What follows is presented in a standard format. Next to a large picture of the bottle, there is information on the brand: who owns it; where it is produced (because not all brands are as clear about that as they might be, and it's not unreasonable that you should know where your gin is actually made); what other variants are offered; and where to find more information (almost without exception the brands all have their own websites). There then follows my entirely personal description of what interested me about the particular product: it may be the people, the story, the history, the production method, the packaging or, sometimes, even the taste.

I have not offered scores. These are only ever one man's opinion and I doubt that mine are consistent over time. You may assume that I found the gin drinkable at the very least, otherwise it would not have been included (and there were some that failed at the very first sip) but I don't want my personal preferences and judgements to influence your decision to try any one of these products.

It strikes me that right now there is a great energy pulsing through the world of gin and that this is as good a time as any to learn about it and simply enjoy it. Above all, there is a freshness about gin today that I find extraordinarily invigorating.

I hope that feeling is evident, and that you share it.

And finally, please remember the words of the American writer Roy Blount, Jr: 'A good heavy book holds you down. It's an anchor that keeps you from getting up and having another gin and tonic.'

Time then for our 101 gins.

Photo: Jared Brown

Botanicals ready for distilling at Sipsmith (juniper berries, bottom left).

1

58 GIN

BRAND OWNER: Mark Marmont

DISTILLERY: Hackney Downs Studios, London

WEBSITE: www.58gin.com

VISITOR CENTRE: By arrangement

AVAILABILITY: Limited

OTHER VARIANTS: None

I thought it would be nice to begin with the UK's newest gin brand (at least, at the time of writing it's the newest – by the time this makes it into print there will be several more trying to make their way in the world). 58 also stands as a great example of the new wave of small operations trying to find a gap in the market; in many ways typifying how gin is changing and why it's the most exciting thing on the world spirits scene right now. I know that's a big claim, but read on – by gin number 101, I believe you'll be convinced.

It's the brainchild of Mark Marmont, who describes himself as 'an avid cocktail lover'. He makes just sixty to seventy bottles of gin at a time in a tiny copper pot still in his own private distillery in Hackney Downs Studios, located in one of the trendier parts of London. Mark did most of the work on the fit-out himself. With a laboratory background, following a year of experimentation and, as he says himself, 'trial and error', and lots of distilling courses he launched 58 with two trial batches in January 2015.

As a cocktail lover Mark was fortunate to spend some time living at 58 Colebrooke Row in Angel where he had Tony Conigliaro's The Bar With No Name at number 69 (this gentleman and bar are legendary in cocktail circles). After sampling many cocktails and realising that the classics are gin-based, he decided to 'investigate' distilling further: before long, 58 was born. Sometimes the research for this kind of project is brutally demanding and requires a very special level of dedication and focus. But sometimes it's just great fun.

A 1920s-style logo was developed by Mo Coppoletta, a tattoo artist at The Family Business (again, we're talking a seriously on-trend guy), as an ode to moonshine and prohibition, and turned into a finished label in the Hackney Downs Studio by designers Tinder & Sparks. So there are several themes here that exemplify the wave of contemporary gins: a genesis in cocktails; extraordinarily small volumes; individual entrepreneurship and hands-on production. But larger distillers can be, in private at least, somewhat dismissive of their smaller rivals, so is 58 any good?

Well, I think so. There will be batch-to-batch variations of course (all part of the fun and not dissimilar to single-cask malt whiskies) but I found it crisp, citrus-y and pleasantly refreshing – great with a dash of Noilly Prat and a lemon peel.

NO. 209

BRAND OWNER:	Distillery 209, San Francisco
DISTILLERY:	Distillery 209, Pier 50, San Francisco, California, USA
WEBSITE:	www.distillery209.com
VISITOR CENTRE:	Distillery tours available
AVAILABILITY:	Specialists
OTHER VARIANTS:	209 Kosher for Passover Gin

Here's one of the better established American gins, which launched in 2005 but which can legitimately lay some claim to having been born in 1882; which had its stills built in Scotland, modelled on those of a single malt whisky but which itself has its origins in gin distilling; which sits over the sea on a San Francisco wharf and produces one of the few gins certified as kosher for Passover. Intrigued? I certainly was.

The 1882 connection links to the original 'Registered Distillery No. 209' (in the romantic nomenclature of the US Federal Government). It was located on the Edge Hill winery in the Napa Valley, but by the time owner Leslie Rudd identified it, little remained but a fading sign above the iron doors of a hay barn. Rudd and his family went on to restore the site. Unfortunately the size and location of the original distillery building didn't suit their plans for the revival of Distillery No. 209, so they simply built a new one, right on Pier 50 in San Francisco, which is said to be the birthplace of the Gin Martini (though not everyone agrees with that theory).

As for the link to single malt whisky, that's rather more tangible. Determined to obtain one of the finest stills money could buy, Leslie Rudd went to Forsyth's, the renowned Scottish makers (coincidentally, in the same year but on America's other coast, Bluecoat of Philadelphia also went to Forsyth's for their plant). Rudd commissioned an unusually tall twenty-five-foot-high still with a capacity of 4,500 litres — clearly they had ambitious plans — modelled on the stills at Glenmorangie, famously the tallest in Scotland. And why are Glenmorangie's stills so tall? Because in 1843 when the distillery first opened it was fitted out with second-hand gin stills from London, and their distinctive size has been faithfully followed ever since. There you are: Scotland's best-loved single malt whisky owes it all to London gin!

No. 209 has since gone from strength to strength and enjoys a high reputation amongst the bar trade. At 46% it carries plenty of body, without being overpoweringly alcoholic. One prominent online retailer described the quintuple-distilled No. 209 as 'the best gin we've tasted in a very long time . . . the best flavour we've ever encountered for a Gin Martini'.

For me fresh lemon and orange notes stand out, complemented by a wave of peppery juniper.

ADNAM'S COPPER HOUSE

BRAND OWNER: Adnams plc

DISTILLERY: Copper House Distillery,
Southwold, Suffolk

WEBSITE: www.adnams.co.uk

VISITOR CENTRE: Yes

AVAILABILITY: Widespread

OTHER VARIANTS: First Rate

I suppose that if you've been brewing great beer since 1872 and operate more than seventy pubs and an off-licence chain then starting to distil your own range of spirits isn't the greatest leap in the dark. And with your own outlets to provide a ready market it's probably a sound commercial move, yet it took Adnams until 2010 to start making vodka, gin, whisky and a range of liqueurs.

But, as you'd expect from their reputation as brewers, they've made a pretty decent job of it (I've tasted the whisky in development and it's excellent; I haven't the faintest idea about their vodka as I have a special dispensation never to touch the stuff).

Both vodka and gin start life as unhopped beer from the Adnams brewery. A column still is used to produce the vodka that then forms the spirit base for the gin. Botanicals (up to thirteen for the premium First Rate style) are added to the beefy 1,000-litre pot and redistilled with no further use of the columns (there is a very clear explanation of this on the website).

The equipment was all new and state-of-the-art when installed in 2009, which is one advantage of starting from scratch, with decent capital behind you. The result is a clean, very elegant and classic London Dry gin that mixes well and has already collected a number of top awards (though as we shall see, not all awards are to be regarded equally highly).

It is, I would judge, more a classic G&T gin than a cocktail base, with a no-nonsense six botanicals; though hibiscus might be considered a bit 'new wave' there is nothing else in there to upset your inner colonel. The higher-strength First Rate employs an additional eight botanicals but drops the hibiscus, thus making thirteen in all. However, to be honest, I preferred Copper House

If you get the chance to visit Southwold grab it and do not let go. After you've visited the brewery and distillery (there are various tours to take) the town itself is quite charming; the beach huts are fun to ogle (especially after you realise the prices at which they change hands); and the pier is worth the trip on its own. You can get great fish; you're only a few miles from Snape Maltings for some culture; and sitting on the beach at Southwold, gin and tonic in hand, watching the rolling waves and passing clouds is one of the great pleasures in life.

ALDI'S OLIVER CROMWELL

BRAND OWNER:	Aldi Stores Ltd
DISTILLERY:	not disclosed
WEBSITE:	www.aldi.co.uk
VISITOR CENTRE:	Lots of shops – not quite the same though
AVAILABILITY:	Aldi stores
OTHER VARIANTS:	None

What do you think you're doing?' I asked my son, who was making sloe gin. 'You've picked all this nice fruit and now you're sticking some horrid supermarket cheapie in there. I trust you don't expect me to drink that.' Being a bit of a drinks snob.

'No, it's OK actually,' he replied. 'You should try it.' And so I did. And then I had another (you should always listen to your children). And I found it good – really not at all bad.

Try to imagine that this doesn't come in a bottle that's a pallid imitation of a well-known brand leader. Try to forget it costs around a tenner a bottle. Imagine if you will, that it's distilled in a former railway arch in Shoreditch by some bearded hipster sporting an armful of tattoos, and costs at least thirty quid. For a 50cl bottle.

Or run up by a radical extreme cocktail commune in a disused monastery in Oregon using organic juniper gathered by moonlight by barefoot monks. At 3,000 feet.

Or simply decant it into a smarter bottle and then amaze your mates. After a while you'll forget your preconceptions and just enjoy a well-made product that lets the liquid do the talking. It's a lovely light and undemanding product (I don't mean that in any pejorative sense), crisp, refreshing and well balanced.

Aldi's Oliver Cromwell Gin was awarded the only Gold Medal in the standard gin class by *Spirits Business* magazine and, even more impressively, another Gold in the International Spirits Challenge (both 2014). These awards followed a Silver Medal from the 2013 IWSC judges, who are not easily pleased. So you don't have to take my (or my son's) word for it: this really is much, much better than the price and packaging would suggest.

If I was being picky I'd like to see the strength somewhat higher, but then I have to remember the price. For the money you can pour with a liberal hand. This looks even more impressive if you have poured it into a trendier bottle and your guests think they're getting the £30 stuff. Believe me, they will.

There's something else you should know about Aldi: its white chocolate is utterly delicious. I realise that's got nothing whatsoever to do with gin, but it's a good tip.

5

ANCIENT MARINER

BRAND OWNER: The Hebridean Liqueur
Company, Helensburgh, Argyll

DISTILLERY: Thames Distillers, Timbermill
Distillery, Clapham, London

WEBSITE: www.hebrideanliqueurs.co.uk

VISITOR CENTRE: No

AVAILABILITY: Limited

I've got to admit I'm a sucker for unusual packaging – and, even in the crowded market of new gins, this stands out. The name, of course, comes from Coleridge's famous poem. Well, if you studied English beyond a fairly basic level, it's famous – if not, the reference is entirely wasted on you. Go and find it on the web, but be warned: it's not the easiest thing he wrote and it does go on a bit.

But whoever designed this packaging was clearly inspired by Gustave Doré's handsome illustrations for the poem and used them on the label, hence the engravings that appear on the side and front panels. Again, if you don't know the poem you might wonder why there's a sailing ship and a large seagull to be found there – hint, it's an albatross.

The Hebridean Liqueur Company doesn't actually make this but they are curiously coy about who does, saying only that it's made in London. But there is nothing to be ashamed of. It comes from Thames Distillers in Clapham, who we shall be meeting more than once in this exploration of the darker thickets of the juniper bush.

It describes itself as a 'London Cut Dry Gin', which is a new descriptor for me. It's a classic juniper-forward London Dry, bottled at a healthy 50% abv. The higher strength takes some of the sting off the 50cl bottle size. At around £28 a bottle, that equates to approximately £31 for a standard bottle at 40% abv. Fair value, I'd say, especially if you stick a candle in the neck of the bottle (once empty, obviously).

More importantly, the higher strength maintains the smoothness and oily, mouth-coating effect of the spirit that makes this feel quite luxurious when drunk neat. Ancient Mariner is not the most complex of flavours, but if you prefer a dry gin with citrus hints and plenty of mouthfeel it might float your boat.

Curiously, Samuel Taylor Coleridge had a verse all about ice in his *Rime of the Ancient Mariner*. Would you like to read it? I think you should.

The ice was here, the ice was there,
The ice was all around:
It crack'd and growl'd, and roar'd and howl'd,
Like noises in a swound!

That's probably enough ice. I stoppeth thee no longer for fear you faint away.

ANNO

BRAND OWNER: Anno Distillers Ltd
DISTILLERY: Anno, Marden, Kent
WEBSITE: www.annodistillers.co.uk
VISITOR CENTRE: Yes
AVAILABILITY: Limited
OTHER VARIANTS: None

Anno is part of the new wave of craft distillers, but not entirely typical. It isn't run by some tattooed hipsters but by two more senior (in age and career terms) former scientists from the pharmaceutical industry who have established something of a family enterprise. What's more, they don't appear to be trying to reinvent gin. Rather, they work within the classic parameters while offering something distinctive.

And, to their credit, they appear to have created something a little bit different and unusual for their first offering. To judge by their website they have approached the whole operation with some precision and rigour, first commissioning their own unique still design from Christian Carl and then selecting quite unfamiliar local Kent botanicals to give Anno its own personality and flavour.

The first time that I tried it I thought that under the classic juniper aromas I could detect a slightly salty tang. It's certainly spicy with some sweet citrus hints, but it's also very well balanced and quite elegant in style with a consistent finish. I still thought there was an elusive salty note in there, which was rather intriguing, so I checked the botanicals and found that they use Kentish samphire. Now, according to the distillery, this should lend 'a rather pleasant sweetness about it with fresh grassy notes'. I daresay they're right and I just imagined it, but I was nonetheless rather gratified to make an association with saltiness and then find samphire in there – which is agreeably salty when eaten of course.

Also in the botanical basket – they employ one for the more delicate ingredients – are Kentish hops, lavender and elderflower, along with rose hips, chamomile and three different citrus components. There's a full list of all sixteen on the website, which is a model of clarity and ease of operation by the way.

They've also managed to create a clean, distinctive and appealing look to the bottle with graphics applied directly to the glass in place of a conventional label. The distinctive 'A' symbol is very strong and relates not only to a name derived from the two co-founders (ANdy and NOrman) but is actually taken from an ancient German alchemical text where it was used as the symbol to describe the process of distillation.

I like the link with the early alchemists, proto-scientists who sought to turn base metals into gold, and these Kentish pioneers, applying modern scientific methodology to a time-honoured tradition while investing it with some of their own restless curiosity.

AVIATION

BRAND OWNER: House Spirits
DISTILLERY: House Spirits, Portland, Oregon, USA
WEBSITE: www.aviationgin.com
VISITOR CENTRE: Yes
AVAILABILITY: Specialists
OTHER VARIANTS: None

Here's a New American gin that really polarises opinion. For the most part, people, especially cocktail mixologists, rave about it. It's picked up some prestigious accolades from top magazines and enjoys a generally stellar reputation.

But some folk don't like it. One comment on noted blog site theginisin.com, following a 4.5/5 point review, read: 'I poured mine down the drain. I made a Martini with it and it was so vile, I didn't even eat the olives.' That's pretty damning.

I wouldn't go that far, but I will declare myself in the 'don't care for it' camp. Personally I found it lacked subtlety; it seemed unbalanced with a coarse and unappealing nose, and a crude herbal note overpowered the taste. Of the orange and floral hints detected by other tasters I could find no hint. But – and I can't say this often enough – this is just one person's opinion and it's why you won't find any scores here. Many other judges would disagree quite forcefully and I wouldn't want to put you off trying it. You may love it, in which case I'm perfectly happy we part as friends.

Aviation, to be fair, was an early pioneer in the craft gin movement and deserves a lot of credit for that. It's the creation of a very well-known Seattle mixologist Ryan Magarian in collaboration with the House Spirits distillery in Portland, Oregon. They also make Medoyeff vodka, which is apparently extremely highly rated (don't ask me, I've no idea why anyone drinks vodka in the first place). After a series of trials, they came up with the Aviation recipe, named it after a classic gin cocktail and launched the product in June 2006, since when it has enjoyed international success.

It was part of a deliberate and conscious move away from the classic, juniper-led English gins that have become known as 'American Gin' or 'New Western Dry Gin' (these categories are applied somewhat loosely). To that extent it succeeds quite dramatically, as no mainstream English distiller would look to make something this extreme.

Apart from the particular botanical mix, which includes cardamom, lavender and sarsaparilla, my personal theory is that a major influence on the taste is the fact that House Spirits use a stainless-steel still. For the most part, gin is distilled in copper, and stainless-steel stills are more usually employed in making fruit eaux de vie.

Be that as it may, if you like a forceful, straight-to-the-point gin this may be for you.

8

BEEFEATER DRY

BRAND OWNER:	Pernod Ricard
DISTILLERY:	Beefeater, Kennington, London
WEBSITE:	www.beefeatergin.com
VISITOR CENTRE:	Yes
AVAILABILITY:	Ubiquitous
OTHER VARIANTS:	Beefeater 24, London Garden (distillery exclusive), Burrough's Reserve

Since 2005, when the French drinks giant Pernod Ricard acquired the Beefeater brand and distillery, things have been looking up for this great old brand – for years the last branded flag-carrier for London-distilled London Dry. They've poured both money and love (the latter every bit as important as the cash) into developing both distillery and brand. Their urbane and unflappable master distiller Desmond Payne is clearly loving every moment of this well-deserved highpoint in his distinguished gin career.

But gin lovers have long recognised the quality behind its iconic label (though, as an aside, I do wish the restless young people in marketing would stop messing about with their torrent of 'limited edition' label designs – if it ain't broke, don't fix it). In many ways, this would be the gin I'd recommend to someone who only had room for one gin in their cupboard and was watching the pennies. Frankly, it's great value, and all things considered it's hard to beat for an authentic gin taste. While researching and writing this book I used it as my reference point.

Recently the distillery has benefited from the development of a small but rather handsome visitor centre (£12, but that includes a G&T) which traces the history of gin, with particular emphasis on London's role, naturally. If you're sufficiently interested you can investigate the individual exhibits with the assistance of an iPad, or you can just stroll quickly through to the tasting that awaits. In the inevitable shop you can pick up a bottle of Beefeater's harder-to-find expressions including the premium 24 (45% with extra tea and citrus botanicals), Burrough's Reserve, a 'barrel rested' aged gin distilled in a tiny nineteenth-century copper still, and the distillery exclusive London Garden expression, inspired, or so it is said, by a visit to the Chelsea Physic Garden. That's the one I'd pick if I could only take one home with me, but all have a claim to your wallet.

In recent years there have also been interesting summer and winter limited editions. You might find one in a bar that keeps a decent range of gins. They're well worth trying and, if you're very lucky, there may even be some bottles left in a few specialist outlets.

Ubiquitous it may be but Beefeater is a classic. Until you've tried it you're not really a gin drinker.

BERKELEY SQUARE

BRAND OWNER:	Quintessential Brands
DISTILLERY:	G & J Distillers, Warrington
WEBSITE:	www.berkeleysquaregin.com
VISITOR CENTRE:	No
AVAILABILITY:	Limited
OTHER VARIANTS:	None

The tall and rather languid-looking Berkeley Square (in fiction, the place itself is home to Bertie Wooster) styles itself 'the single malt of gin'. I'm not entirely sure I understand that as kilts and country tweeds would be entirely inappropriate in the heart of London's fashionable West End – something of a stylistic *faux pas,* in fact. But the gin itself – the creation of G & J Distillers' master distiller Joanne Moore – is as elegant in packaging as it is in style.

Like Hendrick's, which is said to have been inspired by the scent of a rose garden, and even more so Beefeater's London Garden, Berkeley Square has its origins in an English herb garden. Moore has added basil, sage, lavender and kaffir lime leaves to create a distinctively light and fragrant gin with herbaceous top notes complementing the more normal gin botanicals.

Sometimes such experimentation can go too far and the product begins to resemble flavoured vodka, or simply some category all on its own. With all the weight of a gin-making tradition dating back to 1761 (and, like all the Quintessential brands out of the old Greenall's distillery, that date features on the packaging), that would have been a step too far but, even while recognisably gin, this is not a product that will appeal strongly to purists.

The production process itself is interesting. The botanicals are placed in a muslin bag and left to steep in the base spirit for twenty-four hours before distillation commences. The distillers themselves describe this stage as similar to a 'bouquet garni' after which distillation is carried on at a languid pace, rather as some dandy might stroll across the gardens at the heart of Berkeley Square itself. The result is that the delicate essential oils in the herbal botanicals are carried over into the spirit, resulting in a most interesting blend of aromatic herbal notes with a traditional gin background.

Some commentators have been rather critical of the packaging and what they consider to be too overt and unsubtle a 'masculine' positioning, going on to compare this unfavourably with Quintessential's Bloom, which in a rather clichéd manner is described as 'feminine'. It is certainly rather mannered but definitely stands out from the pack.

Not a nightingale then, but a peacock proudly strutting for all the world to see. One might imagine its being served at the Drones Club, though Jeeves would doubtless consider it somewhat *nouveau-riche*!

10

BLACK ROBIN

BRAND OWNER: Simply Pure Ltd
DISTILLERY: Tauranga Distillery, Bay of Plenty, North Island, New Zealand
WEBSITE: www.blackrobingin.co.nz
VISITOR CENTRE: No
AVAILABILITY: Limited
OTHER VARIANTS: None

I'm not really sure what fascination endangered species hold for the gin industry but they do seem to have some kind of appeal to gin above all other spirits (though you can buy vodka that helps the snow leopard). Anyway, we have a gin that supports elephant conservation, and here's one which dedicates part of its profits to the critically endangered black robin of New Zealand.

It is, it must be admitted, a remarkably handsome little bird, and I was rather alarmed to read that by 1980 there were only five left. Up to now I must admit to having been ignorant of its fate but now I've all the excuse I need to drink this little-known New Zealand brand (but not at the expense of the elephants, of course; I'll drink to them on alternate evenings).

Actually that's not really necessary. This is a well-made, clean and complex gin well worth your attention. New Zealand isn't known for distilling, though it did have a modest whisky industry there for some years. The Tauranga distillery, situated in the splendidly named Bay of Plenty, is equipped with a German still from Arnold Holstein and makes both this gin and its sister Blue Duck Vodka (guess what, there aren't many of these guys left either).

The master distiller Michael Deinlein can trace his distilling heritage through the family to Oberammergau, Germany, where in the 1930s his relations made herbal liqueurs. Thus, after studying distillation at the University of Stuttgart, Michael and his family set up business and began, naturally enough, by first importing a still from Germany. Black Robin are a little coy about their botanicals, but claim to use 'traditional exotic botanicals with native New Zealand horopito, one of the world's most ancient flowering plants'. Certainly, there is a spicy note wrapped in a citrus component that gives great delicacy and balance to the nose, creating a distinctive, mellow texture with a refreshing fragrance and an elegant and refined finish. It works well as a sipping gin.

The company make much play of the New Zealand heritage, stressing its 'pure' image, and the rarity of the brand and its emblem. It has enjoyed some success in the USA, and, by the time you are reading this, I anticipate it will be available in Europe and the UK, where I fully expect it will find favour – and not just amongst twitchers.

11

BLOOM

BRAND OWNER: Quintessential Brands
DISTILLERY: G & J Distillers, Warrington
WEBSITE: www.bloomgin.com
VISITOR CENTRE: No
AVAILABILITY: Limited
OTHER VARIANTS: Sloe

This is another somewhat avant-garde new gin from Joanna Moore, who is raising some eyebrows amongst traditionalists with her lighter, more perfumed styles (see also *Berkeley Square*). It is said to be 'feminine', presumably because the taste is considered more 'girly', because of the name, and because the bottle has flowers both embossed and printed on it. (*Note:* I'm not saying this, just observing that it has been said.) That might strike you as more than a little patronising, but equally if I remarked that it might be considered a gin for people discovering gin, or who didn't like 'gin', that also seems unduly dismissive. Better move on before I dig myself in any further.

I did notice two things myself, though: first, the gin has the very faintest straw colour and second, it is certified as kosher. The initial impact on the nose is markedly floral and delicate. Some sweetness is evident, and a citrus note. On the palate that develops to suggest fresh orange and then the floral notes come in. More traditional gin flavours, notably juniper, are definitely present but muted. In some ways this parallels the style development of some contemporary American gins: there are some unorthodox botanicals in here such as honeysuckle, chamomile and pomelo (an Asian citrus fruit resembling a sweet grapefruit – I had to look it up so I thought I would save you the trouble). That presumably is the source of the sweet citrus note, which is rather agreeable, and the floral notes are contributed by the chamomile and honeysuckle.

Like the delicate botanicals used in Berkeley Square, these are infused in the wheat-based neutral grain spirit for twenty-four hours before slow and careful distillation. Some care is required in handling these more subtle botanicals and this is where Moore is showcasing her considerable skill as a distiller. Quite why this should make the gin 'feminine' escapes me – but it is noticeable that another quite floral gin, Hendrick's, is also prepared by one of the few other women in a leading role as a master distiller.

Where I do part company with the distillery is in their recommended G&T serve, which uses Fentimans tonic and is garnished with strawberries. The tonic is too pronounced in flavour in my view and tends to overpower the gin, while the use of strawberries is just silly. Stick to something citrus and save the strawberries for pudding, or a Strawberry Gin Smash (if you must).

12

BLUECOAT

BRAND OWNER: Philadelphia Distilling LLC

DISTILLERY: Philadelphia Distilling,
Philadelphia, Pennsylvania, USA

WEBSITE: www.bluecoatgin.com

VISITOR CENTRE: Yes

AVAILABILITY: Specialists

OTHER VARIANTS: Also available as Barrel
Finished style

Established as recently as March 2005, Bluecoat Gin is a perfect example of the new contenders that are revitalising gin's image – and taste. Using their own custom-designed still, which was handmade for them in Scotland, Philadelphia Distilling have aimed from the start to make what they call American Dry Gin, in a style that is all their own. For a small start-up the company have enjoyed some considerable success and, though they concentrate on the US market, supplies have made it to the UK, and I have even encountered the distinctive blue bottle in a bar in Jerez, Spain (where they do know and love their gin).

The product starts as neutral grain spirit, which is then redistilled five times in the pot still. The use of organic American juniper provides an earthy base to the nose and flavour, while the distinctive signature of Bluecoat is a citrus note derived (I believe) from grapefruit peel – though the distiller would neither confirm nor deny my theory.

The company is run by an energetic and committed young team, enthusiastic enough to establish Pennsylvania's first legal distillery since Prohibition, though others have now followed in their footsteps. Originally based in an industrial unit on the edge of the city, at the time of writing the company was about to move all their distilling and bottling operations to a new, larger site in downtown Philadelphia in the historic waterfront district where a visitor centre will be opened and it will be possible to retail their products direct to the public and offer distillery tours – vital promotional activity for a company of this scale, where bottles are frequently hand-sold on a personal basis.

The Bluecoat name emphasises the distinctively American nature of this gin, being based on the nickname of the militia of the American War of Independence (or Revolutionary War, as the beastly colonists insist on calling it), hence the company's slogan 'Be Revolutionary'.

It's very far from revolting though, and even a true Brit can enjoy Bluecoat's cleansing, refreshing taste and 47% abv strength. The Barrel Finished style is a small-batch release, aged in American oak barrels for three months, which are used only twice. I find the slightly fuller flavour works agreeably well in a Negroni.

With new distilling capacity coming on stream output will increase and I hope we will see more of Bluecoat in international markets.

13

BOMBAY EAST

BRAND OWNER:	Bacardi
DISTILLERY:	Bombay Spirits Company, Laverstoke, Hampshire
WEBSITE:	www.bombaysapphire.com
VISITOR CENTRE:	Yes
AVAILABILITY:	Widespread
OTHER VARIANTS:	Original Dry, Sapphire, Amber (duty-free), Star of Bombay and limited distillery-only editions

Because these entries are organised in strict alphabetical order, you will need to turn the page if you want to read about Bombay Sapphire – but don't go away, because this close relative is every bit as interesting and, as it's quite new, probably something you don't know about. But you should.

We can thank the American sweet tooth and their (generally) fairly nasty tonic waters for the arrival of East. This is the first-ever variant of Bombay Sapphire and began life in a 2011 test market in some US states, with the aim of improving the quality of the G&T in the land of the free.

The problem is that much American tonic is sweetened with corn fructose syrup and has a relatively low quinine content. As a result, we Brits don't like it. To combat the excessively cloying effect of this stuff, East is bottled at 42% abv, and the extra alcohol definitely aids flavour delivery. Then, to the Bombay's standard juniper, citrus, angelica, orris root, coriander, liquorice, cassia bark, almonds, cubeb berries and West African grains of paradise recipe the distillers have added two new botanicals, Thai lemongrass and Vietnamese black peppercorns.

My goodness, it makes a difference. The peppers crackle on the palate for a spectacular opening delivery of spicy heat but the lemongrass then calms down the mouthfeel with its own distinctive note of green citrus. After a few minutes in the glass you can begin to see the family resemblance to Sapphire, but with the extra fiery heat of the peppers and greater complexity, weight and mouthfeel.

The test markets were evidently deemed a success because East is now a permanent part of the Bombay line-up and available on some UK supermarket shelves and in specialist outlets. At first sight the price tag of £44 or so looks rather high, but bearing in mind this is for a litre bottle at 42% it compares favourably with other premium gins, at the equivalent of around £31 for a standard bottle.

I'd expect this to be finding favour here in the UK with mixologists. Given the superior quality of (most) UK tonic, its main role may be in cocktails where the more assertive flavour will carry the flag for gin against the other ingredients.

Incidentally, there is a rather charming little promotional film on YouTube describing the two new botanicals which is worth the few minutes of your time that it will take to watch.

14

BOMBAY SAPPHIRE

BRAND OWNER: Bacardi

DISTILLERY: Bombay Spirits Company,
Laverstoke, Hampshire

WEBSITE: www.bombaysapphire.com

VISITOR CENTRE: Yes

AVAILABILITY: Widespread

OTHER VARIANTS: Original Dry, East, Amber
(duty free), Star of Bombay and
limited distillery-only editions

Like a number of other currently fashionable gins, Bombay Sapphire relies on its retro-style packaging to persuade us it's been around for ages. In one sense it has, in that the base recipe (as used in the Original Dry variant) dates back to 1761 when it was known as Warrington Dry Gin. It did not appear in its Bombay guise until 1960, and Sapphire, which added two botanicals to the recipe, was launched only in 1987.

It has a decent claim to saving the entire gin category, here and in the USA. A new wave of innovative bartenders, led by the legendary Dick Bradsell (inventor of the Bramble cocktail and mentor to today's tattooed 'mixologists'), picked up on Sapphire's light, fresh and delicate nose and taste, and began to look at gin in an exciting new way.

It took a little while for this to gather momentum but a number of competitors followed, chief amongst them Hendrick's. Today, it seems that new gins, ultimately inspired by Sapphire, appear almost weekly.

In 1997 the brand was acquired by Bacardi. Until 2014 production remained at Warrington, where it was distilled under contract by G&J Greenall, but today it has its own home at the splendid Laverstoke Mill, where a magnificent visitor centre has been built. I'll simply urge you to go without delay.

There you can stroll through the very attractive grounds; gasp at the soaring glasshouses designed by Thomas Heatherwick; learn all about botanicals; design your own cocktail; but, best of all, see the highly unusual Carterhead stills which aim to preserve the fresh character of the botanicals through the vapour infusion method of distilling. The result is a subtle and delicate spirit, which, though light in character, does not lack for complexity or charm. Production has been greatly expanded by the multi-million pound move to Laverstoke but great care has been taken to ensure absolute continuity of flavour.

Today, there are a number of variants. Original Dry has been relaunched in the UK, but at the reduced strength of 37.5% abv – a mistake in my view as it drinks disappointingly thin. What you really want is the export strength Sapphire (47%) as found at the airport, which is a superbly rewarding component of a good cocktail, or the exotic East with its beguiling pepper and lemongrass notes.

Then you can raise a glass to the gin which, almost single-handedly, rescued gin!

15

BOTANIST

BRAND OWNER: Bruichladdich Distillery Ltd
(Rémy Cointreau)
DISTILLERY: Bruichladdich, Islay
WEBSITE: www.thebotanist.com
VISITOR CENTRE: Yes
AVAILABILITY: Specialists
OTHER VARIANTS: None

This is what happens when a small, rather isolated whisky distillery that is not without a sense of its own importance makes gin. It's lovely!

The Botanist is made on Islay by Bruichladdich self-styled 'progressive Hebridean distillers'. They do bang on a bit about how they're different from everyone else – though it's also fair to acknowledge that in many ways they are. Their near-obsessive fans have awarded them cult status, despite the distillery and brands having been sold in July 2012 to the French group Rémy Cointreau. In recent years they've shed the *enfant-terrible* pose, which was getting a trifle wearing (at least I thought so) and have matured somewhat.

But they still do fun, unexpected and offbeat things, and for that we may forgive them a lot. Such an attitude lay behind their last-minute recovery of one of the very few surviving true Lomond stills left anywhere in the world shortly before it was fated to end as scrap. The Lomond still was originally designed in the late 1950s as a sort of a compromise between a pot still and a column still and was intended for Scotch whisky. For all sorts of reasons it never really worked satisfactorily and, like the dustbin it resembles, was destined for the waste-basket of whisky history.

However, Bruichladdich's master distiller Jim McEwan realised that if run very slowly it could be ideal for making gin. As the distillery was casting around for new, cash-generative products gin was duly made. But, ever curious, McEwan adapted the still to include a separate container for the botanicals (sourced, of course, uniquely on Islay) and thus worked the Lomond apparatus as a sort of hybrid Carterhead. It's not, let it be said, a particularly good-looking piece of kit. In fact, the distillery have affectionately named it Ugly Betty and painted a rather voluptuous lady onto the top of the column (she's not at all ugly).

As for the gin itself, they first use a fairly standard range of botanicals which are infused with the base spirit and then augment these by passing the vapour through a further twenty-two more delicate island botanicals. The result is a complex, robust yet floral gin of great charm. Rémy Cointreau bought Bruichladdich for their single malt whisky – they may come to find that this was the real bargain.

16

BOXER

BRAND OWNER:	Green Box Drinks Ltd
DISTILLERY:	The Langley Distillery, Langley Green, Warley, West Midlands
WEBSITE:	www.boxergin.com
VISITOR CENTRE:	No
AVAILABILITY:	Specialists
OTHER VARIANTS:	None

You think this is called Boxer because there's a picture of a boxer on the bottle, don't you? Well, it might be . . . but I have another theory. It may just be that it's because it comes *in a box*. Clever, eh?

Not for you and me, you understand; we just get it in a bottle, like any old other gin, and, as you'd expect, there is indeed an illustration of two strapping fellows engaged in fisticuffs right there on the front. But if you run a bar and order Boxer, the first order comes conventionally packaged but your second and subsequent orders arrive as a 4.2-litre bag in a box (like a wine box but bigger – 4.2 litres is the equivalent of the trade's standard six-bottle case). Why?

Well, Green Box Drinks point out that producing a new glass spirits bottle produces 630g of CO_2, and the amount of energy saved by refilling one bottle could power a 100-watt light bulb for eleven hours. The box of Boxer reduces packaging by 95%, they say, transported weight by 45% and transported volume by 63%. All you have to do as the bar owner is keep your empties, carefully refill them (there's a panel on the box where you note how many bottles have been drawn off from the bag), and sit back luxuriating sanctimoniously in a sense of your green virtue. I'm not aware of any other company doing this but it may be a trend that we will see more of in the future.

However, it may be green, but is it any good? Well, if you like a pronounced juniper hit on your gin, then yes it is. Boxer separately distil fresh wild juniper berries at source in the Himalayas and cold-press their bergamot peel and add these extracts to a classic London Dry gin distilled by Langley's of Birmingham (their renowned 'Angela' still is in action here). This means it may only be described as a 'distilled gin' but it ensures a very fresh, forceful and vibrant delivery of the key flavours, which are long-lasting and stand up well to dilution with tonic or in a cocktail.

Sipped neat, the flavours in Boxer are perhaps too assertive, so this is something of a heavyweight amongst gins – to borrow a memorable phrase, it floats like a butterfly but stings like a bee.

Meanwhile, don't forget about Langley's who we shall meet again. They're an important part of gin's revival.

17

BRIGHTON

BRAND OWNER:	Brighton Spirits Company
DISTILLERY:	The Urchin, Hove
WEBSITE:	www.brightongin.com
VISITOR CENTRE:	You could visit The Urchin
AVAILABILITY:	Specialists
OTHER VARIANTS:	None

The late, great Keith Waterhouse, a long-time resident, once memorably declared that 'Brighton has the air of a town helping the police with its inquiries'. It certainly carries a certain raffish manner, an insouciant attitude and a tawdry glamour that for years marked it out as the place to go for a dirty weekend, or perhaps for ill-matched couples needing to provide sham proof of adultery to obtain a divorce.

Again and again this image occurs in books: from *Pride and Prejudice* by way of *Vanity Fair*, *Brighton Rock* and *Sugar Rush* Brighton acts as a counter-point to London, a veritable den of iniquity, sexual excess and casual violence. Not, I hasten to add, that anything at all exciting has ever happened to me on my all too fleeting visits ('and a jolly good thing, too' adds Mrs Buxton).

Gin seems Brighton's natural partner; what else would you drink on some illicit liaison than Mother's Ruin? So it's perhaps surprising that no one has thought to launch a Brighton Gin until now. Even if it were distilled somewhere else Brighton's glitzy allure would surely have exercised a fascination for even the most *outré* of drinkers and injected a *soupçon* of hitherto unsuspected debauchery into the image of the most drably respectable of provincial chartered accountants. But it seems not, so it fell to a group of five Brighton chums to make the first move and distil their very own gin beside the seaside.

So, with their second-hand still, Kathy Caton, former restaurateur, Dr Ian Barry, physicist turned distiller, Helen Chesshire, first lady of drinks PR, Jonathan Ray, drinks journalist, and one-time brewery and coffee entrepreneur Nigel Lambe decided it had to be done. Loving Brighton as they do, the cheery labelling, with its hints of the fairground, has been inspired by the city itself and the distinctive Brighton seafront blue that appears on railings and bus shelters. Was that risky or simply *risqué*?

Their first run of 400 bottles apparently flew off the shelves. The aim is to build local support and then expand, though by the time this reaches the bookshops I fully expect that this crisp citrus-led gin, with its secret botanicals (though they do admit to fresh orange, angelica, lime and the liver-cleansing milk thistle), will have achieved success far from the seaside.

Finally, then, something you can bring home from London-by-the-Sea that you can safely share with your mother-in-law.

18

BROKER'S

BRAND OWNER:	Broker's Gin Ltd, London
DISTILLERY:	The Langley Distillery, Langley Green, Warley, West Midlands
WEBSITE:	www.brokersgin.com
VISITOR CENTRE:	No
AVAILABILITY:	Specialists
OTHER VARIANTS:	Export Strength

Does anyone still wear a bowler hat? Isn't the little plastic hat on top of this bottle, and even the name, simply a bit of a gimmick? Well, yes, but then the company themselves shamelessly admit that this is 'a brand with personality and playfulness; a quirky marketing approach'.

And what's wrong with a bit of fun, you might ask. At under twenty quid this would make a splendid present (I wouldn't turn it down). If you splash out just a little more, you can afford their 47% export strength but check the label carefully if that's not what you want; they are very similarly packaged and easily confused (until you start drinking, that is).

But is the gin any good, I hear you cry. Well, if awards are anything to go by, then yes it is. My bottle came with a little leaflet proudly emblazoned with the unambiguous words 'World's Best Gin' that inside listed a string of medals going back to 2007. If you're not convinced, the website has a longer list going back to 2000. On top of this impressive claim, they go on to assert that Broker's has won more top awards in international competitions over the last ten years than any other gin.

Others might dispute that, but the problem here for the unwitting consumer is that brands have entered into a sort of arms race and, spotting an opportunity, lots of new awards have sprung up, happy to collect the entry fees and dish out gongs. Not all awards are of equal merit – you wouldn't consider a win in the one hundred yards at a school parents' day to match Olympic gold – and the same applies to drinks awards.

Not, I rush to say, that Broker's is anything other than a completely splendid and very fine libation, especially if you like a straightforward, traditional classic gin which this is, most definitely and unapologetically. Distilled by Langley's in 'Angela', a good old John Dore pot still of a century and more's vintage, just ten botanicals are used. No surprises and nothing 'weird and wonderful' in the list; after all, as they say themselves, 'We believe our forefathers did an unbeatable job perfecting gin recipes over many hundreds of years.'

That seems fair enough. So, if you're looking for a slightly offbeat gift for a gin connoisseur that won't break the bank look no further. Broker's is it: you can take your hat off to it.

19

BURLEIGH'S

BRAND OWNER: 45 West Distillers

DISTILLERY: Nanpantan, Loughborough, Leicestershire

WEBSITE: www.burleighsgin.com

VISITOR CENTRE: Yes

AVAILABILITY: Specialists

OTHER VARIANTS: Export Strength, Distiller's Cut

I've just noticed that a lot of gins begin with the letter 'B'. Before you ask, I haven't the faintest idea why this is, but look how long it's taken us just to get here. What's more, Burleigh's is distilled by a chap named Baxter. Call it coincidence if you will, but I think it's fate.

He appears to be moving backwards from the letter 'C'. That's not a cryptic clue, merely a reference to the fact that Burleigh's master distiller Jamie Baxter began work at Chase Distillery, then moved on to City of London and continues in a consultancy capacity helping other smaller distillers get started.

Right now, he's got his own distillery (with custom-designed still, naturally) at the wonderfully named Nanpantan and, with partners Graham Veitch, Tim Prime and Phil Burley, has created Burleigh's. Now, you might assume that it's Burleigh's for Mr Burley, but you'd be wrong – the name comes from the distillery's location near to Charnwood Forest and Burleigh Wood nature reserve. As the story goes, Jamie was walking there one day and was inspired by the local botanicals that he found – including silver birch, dandelion, burdock, elderberry and a few secret ingredients as well as some more conventional ones.

As a mark of how fast the new generation of artisan gins are gaining acceptance, only two months after producing its first batch Burleigh's was seen on the shelves of Harrods and the Savoy along with the two Michelin star Hand and Flowers, in Marlow, Buckinghamshire. It's impressive stuff.

As to the signature expression, it's a fairly classic London Dry, well made and elegant. The nose is crisp, clean and fresh, with juniper and citrus coming through nice and early, an initial hit of juniper and pine with floral and spicy dry notes on tasting, followed by tart orange notes and a warming finish.

And, if you're inspired, you can tap into this expertise, because 45 West offer a full service to help you set up your own distillery, right down to sending in a 'flying distiller' every few batches once you've got started, just to hold your hand until everything is going smoothly. So they're not frightened of competition, it would seem, but some of their competitors might get a surprise, especially if they go down to the woods today. Making gin is no picnic!

20

BURROUGH'S RESERVE

BRAND OWNER: Chivas Brothers
DISTILLERY: Beefeater, Kennington, London
WEBSITE: www.beefeatergin.com
VISITOR CENTRE: Yes
AVAILABILITY: Specialists
OTHER VARIANTS: None

You might casually assume that this was simply Beefeater that has spent some time in an old barrel. You might think it's another one of their 'seasonal' limited edition experiments. But think again. This is quite genuinely different, rather innovative and well worthy of its own entry.

On its launch back in 2013 this set folks in the gin world talking. Oak-aged gins had hitherto been the province of small craft distillers. For a major brand, from a highly regarded master distiller, to launch something in this category was a considerable surprise and immediately lent credibility to what had hitherto been a somewhat raffish style. So what is it exactly?

It starts with the original Beefeater recipe, refined by the founder James Burrough in the 1860s, but uses his original copper 'Still Number 12' which came from the first Cale Street, Chelsea, distillery. With a capacity of only 268 litres, it's dwarfed by the stills around it and, in fact, hasn't been used on a regular basis for some years. Because of the different shape, size and construction this little guy produces small batches of spirit with their own intriguing character, harking back in fact to how gin may have tasted more than a hundred years ago.

After distillation, the gin is 'rested' for some weeks in Jean de Lillet oak barrels in the distillery cellars. A very fine, sought-after wine apéritif, much beloved of trendier cocktail folk, Jean de Lillet is only created in vintage years, making it one of the ultimate ingredients for a classic Martini. So naturally its barrels are the optimum resting place for an exceptional gin, and very different in character from the casks normally used to age gin. In fact, the batches are so limited that each bottle of Burrough's Reserve displays a unique batch and bottle number – and that is reflected in a retail price of over £60, making this one of the most expensive gins out there. Is it worth it?

I would say so, provided you don't fill your glass with ice and lemon and then pour some tonic (however good) on top. This is one of those rare gins for sipping slowly and contemplatively. Enjoy the delicate pale colour, explore the complex nose, relish and appreciate the evolving and layered taste, and remember that if it was a single malt whisky it would be twice the price.

Begone beastly Bs: enough of your beatitudes.

CAMBRIDGE

BRAND OWNER: Cambridge Distillery

DISTILLERY: The Cambridge Distillery, Silver Street, Cambridge

WEBSITE: www.cambridgedistillery.co.uk

VISITOR CENTRE: By appointment

AVAILABILITY: To order

OTHER VARIANTS: Cambridge Gin, Japanese, Anty

Let's assume you've tried all the gins in this book, and more. Despite this rigorous and demanding research something isn't quite right – you simply haven't found the gin that does it for you; there's some fleeting, elusive flavour that commercial gins simply haven't captured. Or perhaps you want something utterly exclusive, bespoke and personalised. You want your own gin.

The help you clearly need is at hand. In his tiny Cambridge Distillery Will Lowe will create it for you. Cambridge already make their own eponymous gin (find it in Selfridges) as well as Japanese Gin and Anty Gin (yes, they distil ants to go in it) but for the ultimate gin experience – the company call it 'gin tailoring' – they will sit down with you and create precisely and exactly your own personal gin to your own specification. Then they lock the recipe away in a safe, and when further supplies are required only you and Will Lowe know the secret.

Gin tailoring involves a ninety-minute one-to-one session in which you'll nose a range of distillates and select those that appeal. A prototype is then made, which you evaluate, and from that the final recipe is developed. After that, you can order the bottles you need, sixty at a time (it claims to be the smallest distillery in Britain, so don't expect to be launching your gin in Tesco any time soon).

Most of the gin tailoring takes place at the distillery in Cambridge but Lowe does go on tour, visiting London, Bath, Manchester and Edinburgh through the year – details and bookings are made through the website. As you may imagine, sessions book up well in advance.

It's not actually a unique service. Edinburgh Gin offer something similar, as do the Ginstitute in London's Notting Hill and the Gin Lab at the City of London Distillery. All are capitalising on the fact that gin can be ready virtually instantly (as opposed to, say, making your own whisky) and a trend for 'experiences' and 'customisation'. The difference is basically that between made-to-measure and bespoke.

Naturally, it comes with a price tag. The London sites mentioned charge around £100 to £125, for which you end up with just one bottle of your private stock. The cost of gin tailoring with Cambridge is £300 and, at the time of writing, they have created more than 900 recipes. *1,001 Gins to Try Before You Die*, anyone?

CAORUNN

BRAND OWNER:	Inver House Distillers
DISTILLERY:	Balmenach, Cromdale, Moray
WEBSITE:	www.caorunngin.com
VISITOR CENTRE:	No
AVAILABILITY:	Specialists
OTHER VARIANTS:	None

An apple a day keeps the doctor away!' Well, that's my excuse. Caorunn (say it 'ka-roon') recommend a slice of red apple in place of the more normal lime or lemon and I think that's probably a first. Is it just a gimmick, though?

Well, if lime or lemon are there to enhance gin's citrus flavours, the fact that Caorunn include the ancient Coul Blush variety of apples in their botanical line-up, alongside six classics such as juniper and coriander, could provide the justification. Mind you, they've got rowanberries in there as well (the trees keep witches away, at least according to Celtic folk tradition – and ever since I planted one I've never had a problem with over-friendly old hags at my front door), and bog myrtle and heather, not to mention dandelion. Quite apart from the fact that dandelion is a pernicious weed, albeit with a pretty flower, I believe we'll draw a veil over its alleged diuretic properties. I'm not at all certain what I'm expected to taste when encountering dandelion, though as we have already noted, it's also used in Burleigh's gin.

By virtue of its parent Inver House Distillers, who have a range of single malt whiskies, Caorunn have achieved wider distribution than many other small gin brands. They've also collected a number of decent awards. What's more interesting is that it's made at Balmenach, a small single malt whisky distillery on Speyside that dates back to 1824, but using a dedicated gin still. Around 1,000 litres of triple-distilled grain spirit are used in each batch, the spirit vapour being passed through a unique copper Berry Chamber that dates to the 1920s. Botanicals are arranged there on four trays and slowly infused in the vapour before being condensed back to spirit.

This somewhat resembles the Carterhead process, in that it relies on the vapours passing over the key botanicals in order to create the desired flavour. The package is a most attractive one, with much emphasis on the number five: five sides; five Celtic botanicals; a five-pointed asterisk decorating the bottle; and so on. Caorunn thus proudly style themselves a 'small-batch Scottish gin' and bottle at 41.8% abv. Though technically this could be described as London Dry it's a measure of the owner's self-assurance and confidence in the Scottish heritage that this takes pride of place on the packaging.

And why not? Great gin was always made in Scotland and Caorunn proudly uphold that tradition.

23

CHASE ELEGANT

BRAND OWNER:	Williams Chase Distillery Ltd
DISTILLERY:	Chase Distillery, Rosemaund Farm, Hereford
WEBSITE:	www.chasedistillery.co.uk and www.williamschase.co.uk
VISITOR CENTRE:	Yes
AVAILABILITY:	Widespread
OTHER VARIANTS:	Extra Dry, Seville Orange, Sloe and Mulberry

Once upon a time a hard-up Herefordshire potato farmer found there was more money making premium crisps than selling spuds, and so Tyrell's Crisps were born. Then this entrepreneurial fellow, one William Chase, discovered small-batch potato vodka and found there was more money in making luxury vodka than premium crisps. It also used up the smaller potatoes that weren't suitable for making crisps. Handy, that.

Enter some venture capitalists who paid £30m (some accounts say £40m) for the crisp company, but he soon fell out with them. Still, no longer hard up, that allowed him to acquire a large yacht, a lot of property and a £3m distillery with a seventy-foot-high rectifying column (it's every bit as tall as it sounds; I went to see it and looking up at it made my neck hurt). Now, I don't know about you, but I like a salty snack with my beverages. However, the venture capitalists, by now no longer the best of friends, didn't agree and so the Tyrell name disappeared from the vodka bottles and Chase Distillery emerged.

Fortunately Chase had got in ahead of the rush to small-brand premium vodkas, was well financed and smartly run by an experienced businessman, and made a fine product, so all went well. Jamie Baxter, whose name you will see several times in this book, was the first distiller. Being based on a farm, Chase grows other things such as apples (this is Herefordshire, after all) and they provide the base for the vodka that they turn to gin. This isn't unique (as the name suggests, Tuthilltown's Half Moon Orchard Gin is also apple based), but it is fairly unusual.

A total of 450 litres of the apple-based vodka is then placed in Ginny, a separate copper pot still with a Carterhead vapour chamber where a pillowcase full of botanicals turns the spirit into gin prior to arriving in the small condenser. The botanicals are conventional enough, other than the addition of hops and fresh apples: fittingly enough, as the distillery buildings were once an experimental hop kiln and the National Association of Cider Makers had a trial orchard here.

At the heart of the Chase success is the fact that this is a family-owned, estate-grown and estate-distilled product. It's bottled on site and Chase proudly proclaim it to be 'field to bottle'. Better still, much of the waste goes to feed their herd of pedigree Hereford cattle. The circle is complete!

24

CHILGROVE

BRAND OWNER:	The Chilgrove Gin Company Ltd
DISTILLERY:	Thames Distillers, Timbermill Distillery, Clapham, London
WEBSITE:	www.chilgrovegin.com
VISITOR CENTRE:	No
AVAILABILITY:	Specialists
OTHER VARIANTS:	None

Once upon a time (you began the last entry that way: *Ed*. I know, but it's to see if they're still awake) when gin was first being made by the Dutch, they used wine for the base spirit.

Chilgrove explain it thus: 'While it is widely known that English gin as we know it today has its roots in sixteenth-century Holland and is derived from the juniper-based drink Jenever, it's a lesser known fact that Jenever was originally made using alcohol distilled from wine. The change to a cereal base occurred as a result of a wine shortage in Holland driven by the significant effects the "Little Ice Age" had on European viticulture coupled with changes in the political landscape.'

That would date the change to around the middle of the sixteenth century when, indeed, winter landscapes suddenly start to appear in Dutch art. Academics have linked the arrival of the Little Ice Age and the consequent agricultural failures in Europe to famines, hypothermia, bread riots and even episodes of witch-hunting. By the seventeenth century the Thames was regularly freezing, and conditions were markedly worse in the Netherlands. So some Dutch courage would certainly have been called for, and, if there was no wine available, then it's entirely feasible that grain would have been used.

Of course, that then became the standard, and today almost all gin is distilled from a neutral grain spirit base. The sole exceptions are Santamanía and Xoriguer from Spain, G'Vine from France and now England's Chilgrove where they maintain that they have simply gone back to first principles to source a superior grape neutral spirit as their starting point, eschewing ever more exotic botanicals.

But using a grape-based spirit for the first time presented some challenges to distiller Charles Maxwell. It was found that some botanicals behave differently – lime, for example, had to be substituted for grapefruit and lemon – and, as you might expect, the spirit has a different, slightly richer mouthfeel (old fogey alert: not all gin drinkers care for the extra richness of these grape-based expressions).

On the nose a grape-y impression is evident (possibly just due to prior knowledge) and the aroma carries sweet juniper notes too. After that, tasting shows juniper and spice, with pine and mint, suggestions of red fruits, and that distinctive oily weight that is the signature of these grape-based gins. Don't be deterred: you really do need to try it to make up your mind.

25

CITADELLE

BRAND OWNER: Cognac Pierre Ferrand

DISTILLERY: Ferrand, Ars, France

WEBSITE: www.citadellegin.com

VISITOR CENTRE: No

AVAILABILITY: Specialists

OTHER VARIANTS: Réserve

Citadelle is made in France, in the heart of the Cognac region, using direct-fired cognac stills. It was one of the first 'artisanal' distillers to produce gin, releasing the first batch of Citadelle in 1995 and the oak aged 'yellow gin' Réserve in 2008.

Cognac distillers Ferrand are limited by law to producing brandy between November and March each year, meaning that the stills traditionally lie idle for six months of the year. That seemed a waste to company owner Alexandre Gabriel, so he decided to put his all-too-still stills to use by making gin in the months he could not produce cognac: 'I always loved the extreme complexity and the finesse that gin offered but was frustrated with what the market had to offer, which was usually too sharp for my taste. My dream was to produce gin with a capital "G" – Gin with some importance.'

So he began to study the distillation methods used to make genièvre – the French ancestor of gin. With the help of a scholar he rummaged through a century-old archive in Dunkirk where, amongst the crumbling papers, they found notes on ancient distillation methods to make gin (some as old as 250 years). A five-year battle to get the necessary permissions then ensued, but we can all be glad that M. Gabriel persisted.

Using nineteen different botanicals, infused for seventy-two hours, distilled for twelve hours using a small (twenty-hectolitre) hammered-copper pot still, and then rested before bottling at 44% Citadelle is a product of great subtlety and sophistication. As they explain: 'few gins are produced in pot stills, and Citadelle is the only gin distilled in a cognac pot still with a naked flame. Distilling gin on an open flame requires a deft touch and far more attention than a column still or steam distillation which is otherwise used. It also means the gin is made in smaller batches, one cask at a time allowing the master distiller to precisely discard the "heads" and "tails" of the distillation, and only keeping the precious, flavourful "heart" of the distillation.'

The oak-aged Réserve is particularly worthy of attention. Each annual batch is clearly dated and represents an evolution of the house style. It's a product made with great care, love and experience, reflected in a complex and rewarding taste that continues to satisfy and evolve to the bottom of the glass. Sipped neat it is a revelation.

CITY OF LONDON

BRAND OWNER:	City of London Distillery Ltd
DISTILLERY:	COLD Bar, 22–24 Bride Lane, London
WEBSITE:	www.cityoflondondistillery.com
VISITOR CENTRE:	Bar
AVAILABILITY:	Limited
OTHER VARIANTS:	None

At the height of the Gin Craze (1720–1751) it has been estimated that in parts of London one house in every four was a gin shop; this in addition to the countless hawkers selling gin on the street. In 1729, when the first Gin Act was passed there were some 1,500 recorded distillers in London alone and, we may safely presume, any number of entirely clandestine operations.

So our ancestors would not have been remotely surprised to step into a pub and find a distillery there. That essentially describes the City of London Distillery, which is located in the COLD Bar on Bride Lane, just off Fleet Street. Stepping down to the basement bar comes as a total revelation to today's drinker. On the one hand is the splendidly stocked bar, complete with period décor and gin ephemera, and directly opposite, behind a plate-glass window, are the stills, nicknamed Jennifer and Clarissa.

They were first operational in December 2012, under the watchful eye of distiller Jamie Baxter (formerly of Chase Distillery and now masterminding Burleigh's operations, when not consulting for eager new craft distillers). Distilling and bottling of COLD gin takes place here, making the bar a curiosity in its own right as the only manufacturing business in the City of London. I'm told that, as such, it attracts banking and finance types who creatively expense their visit as 'research into manufacturing industry'!

The bar itself has been through several incarnations. As a bright and ambitious young graduate my first place of employment was not far from Bride Lane. I wondered aloud one day why the company's senior directors frequently retired at lunchtime and returned late in the afternoon rather 'tired and emotional'. In tones that brooked no further enquiry I was told that they had 'been to a meeting' at the City Golf Club – in actual fact, the self-same licensed premises that today house the COLD distillery. Had it been there then I doubt they would ever have returned to their desks.

The gin itself is now available at some retailers and in other smart bars. It's a clean, crisp spirit with a pronounced citrus note – very tasty! At the COLD Bar you can take a tasting tour, make your own personal bottle in their trial still, or even commission 200 bottles of your own bespoke creation – a contemporary twist on an important part of London's gin heritage.

27

CORK

BRAND OWNER:	Irish Distillers Ltd (Pernod Ricard)
DISTILLERY:	Midleton, Cork, Ireland
WEBSITE:	www.irishdistillers.ie
VISITOR CENTRE:	Yes, but primarily for whiskey
AVAILABILITY:	Widespread in Irish Republic; elsewhere limited
OTHER VARIANTS:	None

I didn't want to entirely fill this book up with brands created in the last decade. Exciting though the gin revival undoubtedly is, I thought it important to give space to some of the unsung and unfashionable brands that nonetheless kept the gin flag flying through the period when it wasn't at all trendy.

And there is probably no better example than Irish Distillers' Cork gin. Created in 1793, with its recipe first recorded five years later, Cork gin is today regarded by its owners as a 'heritage brand'. To put that more bluntly, it's a cash cow – despite selling almost one in every two gins served in the Irish Republic it gets very little in the way of time and attention and is left pretty much to its own devices. There was an attempt about ten years ago at a premium version, Cork Crimson, but that appears to have been withdrawn with little fanfare. Shame: perhaps not a propitious moment; had it only held on for a few more years it could possibly have benefited from today's market.

There appears to have been a Blue Label export strength as well, but that also seems to have disappeared without trace. You'd think that Irish Distillers' parent Pernod Ricard, having made such a good job of Beefeater and Plymouth, would apply a little of their undoubted gin marketing skills here and do more with this. Or get their pot still whiskey team on it – if they can reinvigorate Cork as well as they have breathed new life into pot still whiskey there is still hope for this faithful old servant.

It's hard though to pretend that this is much more than an everyday workhorse of a gin; it's priced and packaged accordingly, yet makes a perfectly serviceable standby, especially if you favour something with a forceful taste profile.

Technically, this is a cold-compounded gin (i.e. the botanical extracts or essences are simply mixed with neutral grain spirit, not distilled), which I wouldn't normally recommend. Distilled gins are more complex and generally considered to be higher quality; what's more this is bottled at a modest 37.5% abv. But half the gin drunk in Ireland must count for something, and I couldn't pass by such a long heritage without at least drawing this to your attention, even if you drink it only on Saint Patrick's Day!

CORSAIR

BRAND OWNER:	Corsair Artisan LLC
DISTILLERY:	Corsair Artisan Distillery, 400 East Main Street, Bowling Green, Kentucky, USA
WEBSITE:	www.corsairartisan.com
VISITOR CENTRE:	Yes
AVAILABILITY:	Limited
OTHER VARIANTS:	Barrel Aged, Genever, Old Tom, Steampunk

Corsair (look it up; it means 'privateer' or 'pirate' – a name they didn't choose by accident) Artisan (we know what that means and again I'm sure it wasn't idly chosen) claim to make 'Small Batch Ultra Premium Booze for Badasses'. I'm not sure if I really qualify.

But you'll have gathered from that and the *Reservoir Dogs*-style label (they use variations of it for everything that they produce) that there's a certain consciously iconoclastic attitude here. It's not some surly, adolescent snarling, however; behind the pose there is a well-thought-out appeal to the market and a deep commitment to experimentation and innovation in distilled spirits. One of the partners has an MBA, so you can be sure that some shrewd thinking went on before they opened their doors.

They've been going since early 2008, and gin was one of their first products. Corsair fairly rapidly found favour with opinion formers in the cocktail bar community and have subsequently picked up a barrow-load of awards (for such an anti-establishment renegade bunch they're surprisingly keen on external validation of their efforts).

Founders Darek Bell and Andrew Webber, both still in their thirties, have certainly made a mark on the spirits business. Bell has even written a book, *Alt Whiskeys*, which has had a major influence on the craft distilling sector. Their other facility, in Tennessee, actually houses an old pre-Prohibition gin still, but today all their white spirits are made on a small (fifty US gallons, so it means around forty-two in UK measures: US gallons are smaller than British ones) still from Vendome, a well-known US manufacturer, which is housed in their Kentucky plant.

They describe Corsair as a 'gin-head-style American gin', referring to the fact that the botanicals are suspended in a vapour basket and thus the spirit vapour passes through the botanicals, in a manner similar to a Carterhead still.

At 44% it's a forceful, but not aggressive or unduly assertive, spirit with lots of citrus (think orange compote) and pine on the nose, a full body with spicy herbs, nuts, lemongrass and fresh celery on the palate. Some tasters detect savoury notes, likening the aroma to broth, but that missed me entirely. Served with a little iced water it's an agreeable sipping gin in the 'New American' style and it makes a mean Martini.

29

COTSWOLDS

BRAND OWNER:	Cotswolds Distillery Company
DISTILLERY:	Cotswolds Distillery, Stourton, Shipston-on-Stour
WEBSITE:	www.cotswoldsdistillery.com
VISITOR CENTRE:	Yes
AVAILABILITY:	Limited
OTHER VARIANTS:	None

If you look hard enough you'll find two 'Cotswold Gins' out there. Confusing, isn't it? Well, this one is actually distilled in the heart of the Cotswolds in a rather lovely distillery in a charmingly bucolic setting.

The operation was established by former financier Daniel Szor. (Who says something good can't become of such people? Would that all bankers took up some small craft industry and got their hands dirty.) He saw the light some years ago, abandoned the City and followed his dream of making whisky in the Cotswolds with locally grown and malted barley. Good idea, but tough on the cash flow.

So, using a bespoke top-quality German still, Cotswolds added gin to their line-up – and very good it is too. Perhaps that's not surprising: they have actually gone to the lengths of employing a botanist to advise on local botanicals, and they aim to grow many of the rarer botanicals on site (I told you it was charming).

The distinctive, non-standard botanicals include Cotswolds lavender and bay leaf, grapefruit and lime which are contained in a Carterhead-style basket rather than being macerated and distilled with the base spirit. The finished product is not chill filtered. This may result in a slight cloudiness when ice is added but contributes to a smooth and rounded mouthfeel, which goes very well alongside the citrus and pine-juniper notes which are very much to the fore here.

It's a product that works well in a conventional G&T but is also a fine cocktail base. The distillery themselves suggest the Corpse Reviver No. 2. That's a splendid libation which, in the words of the immortal Harry Craddock is 'to be taken before 11 a.m., or whenever steam and energy are needed'. But don't forget his cautionary note: 'Four of these taken in swift succession will quickly unrevive the corpse again.'

The level of investment here – on distillery, offices and visitor centre, packaging, not to mention the youthful and enthusiastic team – speaks of a deep and lasting investment by Szor who claims not to have an 'exit strategy' (you might imagine at first glance that a call from a big distiller is hoped for, but I genuinely believe this isn't the case). It's illustrative of the fact that the 'craft distilling' sector is growing up very fast and, in its better exponents, more than capable of producing distinctive and interesting products that add variety to our drinking repertoire.

CREAM

BRAND OWNER:	The Worship Street Whistling Shop
DISTILLERY:	Prof. Cornelius Ampleforth's Compounding Works, Tunbridge Wells
WEBSITE:	www.masterofmalt.com
VISITOR CENTRE:	No, but the Whistling Shop mixes a mean cocktail.
AVAILABILITY:	Limited
OTHER VARIANTS:	None

Imagine some scientists attempting to bring back an extinct species – a mammoth, for example, or Steller's sea cow (this unfortunate creature lasted just twenty-seven years after European hunters discovered its remaining habitat). Well, Cream Gin is – or rather was – an extinct species until noted London cocktail guru Ryan Chetiyawardana (then working in the Worship Street Whistling Shop) grew increasingly interested in early illustrations of gin palaces where he saw references to Old Tom and Cream Gin. He knew what Old Tom was but was perplexed and intrigued by Cream Gin, as well he may have been. Eventually he concluded that this 'alluded to the fact that it was probably gin mixed with cream and sugar and left in barrels to soften the harshness of the gin'.

Presumably it wasn't the very best gin, and presumably this product didn't have much of a shelf life, but Chetiyawardana and colleagues saw no reason why they couldn't bring this lost drink back to life – to save it from extinction as it were.

From there it was but a short step to making it, initially only for the bar where it was used in one of their signature drinks, the Black Cat's Martini (a simple mix of dry vermouth with Cream Gin; essentially a Dry Martini but garnished with a radish). It proved popular; so much so that they formed a partnership with the team at Professor Cornelius Ampleforth's who were able to produce it in larger quantities.

To update this classic idea, the newly resurrected Cream Gin has been cold distilled using fresh cream as a botanical (the equivalent of 100ml cream per bottle!) to capture its flavour in a perfectly clear spirit. Because the cream is never heated during the distillation process, there are no 'burnt' or 'off' flavours, and, unlike its Victorian antecedent, Cream Gin has the same shelf life as any other distilled spirit. It may sound strange, but something of the sort works in Bailey's Irish Cream so it's not as outrageous an idea as first it may seem.

This will only ever be a highly specialised product with limited applications but it's actually a perfectly decent gin, albeit with an unusual mouthfeel that I can only describe as . . . creamy. Not everyone will want something this specific, but if you need a really creamy gin in your life, then this is unique. That alone makes it interesting and well worth trying at least once.

31

CREMORNE COLONEL FOX'S

BRAND OWNER:	Cask Liquid Marketing Ltd
DISTILLERY:	Thames Distillers, Timbermill Distillery, Clapham, London
WEBSITE:	www.caskliquidmarketing.com
VISITOR CENTRE:	No
AVAILABILITY:	Limited
OTHER VARIANTS:	Sloe

I was at first, I will admit, a little reluctant to admit this to the 101. After all, that's quite an honour and here is yet another contract-distilled product (from the indefatigable Charles Maxwell) that means some new small distillery has missed out. And, at first sight, the backstory of the brand is, well, a trifle contrived. And even if the label intrigues it's a pretty boring bottle.

And then I started to dig deeper. Despite my initial scepticism I was drawn in, initially by that very strange label with its starchy Victorian regimental figure with a fox's head. His zoomorphic form at first reminded me of an ancient Egyptian deity. Perhaps, I conjectured, Colonel Fox was a therianthrope. What, I wondered, would his brothers-in-arms make of this? What if he made a mess in the mess?

It turns out that the label was designed by the extraordinarily talented artist and writer Charlotte Cory. Apart from having a doctorate in Medieval Literature she has written three novels and several radio productions for the BBC. That's when she isn't creating a remarkable post-Darwinian world inhabited by bizarre, surrealist creatures such as the Colonel. Curiously, Hendrick's have done similar promotional work with the strangely similar artwork of Dan Hillier. Look them both up – it's worth the effort.

Anyway, Cory's imaginary world collided with elements of the real world in the creation of this brand, launched only in 2012 and which is seen mainly in smarter pubs and clubs. Cremorne Gardens was a real place where I have no doubt the Victorians consumed copious quantities of gin. The recipe comes from the Maxwell family archive but had not been used for many years: the whole *faux*-Victorian theme started to come together, expressed in a classically robust gin that will appeal to traditionalists.

Just how good it is was brought home to me when I learned that in a staff blind tasting at Edinburgh's Bramble Bar (a shrine to the juniper berry) Colonel Fox's was the runaway winner. Frankly, if it's good enough for them I didn't think I could deny it a place in this pantheon.

And there are two clinchers: first of all, the price. This will only set you back around twenty guineas (work it out, young people) – a pretty fair bargain for a Charlotte Cory print. Second of all, it has the best health advisory notice ever: but as I don't want to spoil the fun you'll have to buy a bottle to see what I'm on about.

32

D1

BRAND OWNER:	D. J. Limbrey Distilling Company Ltd
DISTILLERY:	The Langley Distillery, Langley Green, Warley, West Midlands
WEBSITE:	www.d1londongin.com
VISITOR CENTRE:	No
AVAILABILITY:	Limited
OTHER VARIANTS:	None

I'm not being critical when I tell you this is a somewhat two-faced gin, just something of a smarty-pants. As you can see, the bottle features a striking image of a blue skull and the label has been designed to be reversible – it presents two faces. You can have the label and blue skull, as seen opposite, or the skull with a Union Jack flag which makes up the back of the label. Whichever way you turn it, though, you can't escape the macabre image of the death's head. I suspect the eye sockets follow you around the room.

D. J. Limbrey Distilling, like a number of the more recent start-ups, don't actually do any distilling but have the tedious business of actually making a product contracted out elsewhere – in this case to Langley's who make a number of the new-wave gins featured here on behalf of the various brand owners.

The gimmick (sorry, point of difference) with D1 – apart from the ghoulish packaging – is the inclusion of nettles with the botanicals, which we are asked to believe is a 'daring kick'. They were selected by a master tea blender, presumably because nettle blenders are thin on the ground or perhaps because one stung them for his fee. The fulsome tasting notes on the website refer to the nose delivering 'a crest of nettle tailed by apricots with rich blackcurrant airs'.

To be honest, I had some difficulty visualising that, or even working out what it meant, but as I don't know what distilled nettles are supposed to smell like (be honest, do you?) I was at something of a disadvantage. And it didn't seem very fruity either.

Publicity for D1 makes much of the skull motif, which was designed by 'international contemporary artist' Jacky Tsai. The skull is, as you might expect, 'iconic' (line three of his bio). The floral element is part-credited to Alexander McQueen, though, of course, artists have been using this device for centuries and across many cultures. Dürer and Holbein are just two examples that spring to mind from my sketchy knowledge of Western art ('sketchy' knowledge of art – see what I did there?) and Aztec, Mixtec and even Mayan craftsmen were creating such things hundreds of years ago. And, for the love of God, I'm not even going to mention Damien Hirst and his notorious jewel-encrusted skull.

I can't really see the point of this, other than an attempt to create some kind of a shocked reaction. The gin is perfectly inoffensive but, at around £35 to £40, there are better buys, unless the packaging appeals.

33

DARNLEY'S VIEW

BRAND OWNER: Wemyss Malts Ltd

DISTILLERY: Thames Distillers, Timbermill
Distillery, Clapham, London

WEBSITE: www.darnleysview.com

VISITOR CENTRE: No

AVAILABILITY: Limited

OTHER VARIANTS: Spiced Gin

In my line of work I'm exposed to a fair old amount of PR and marketing guff. The theory goes that brands have to have a backstory, some sort of heritage or provenance that will provide emotional engagement for the consumer. There's a whole industry of 'brand consultants' driving BMWs on the strength of this stuff.

Most of the time, when it bears some sort of more or less oblique relationship to the truth, it's harmless enough and sometimes actually tells us something important or relevant about the product. Occasionally though, the spinmeisters get carried away. Consider the following about Darnley's View (launched 2010).

> Scotland, 1565. Mary, Queen of Scots first spies her future husband, Lord Darnley, through the courtyard window of Wemyss Castle, the historic family seat of renowned vintners and spirits merchants, the Wemyss family (pronounced 'weems'). Today, in recognition of this defining moment, they bring you the superbly balanced, hand crafted Darnley's View Gin.

In its way, it's a little masterpiece – the skilful introduction of an entirely spurious heritage and cast of historical characters, little more than merely corroborative detail, intended to give artistic verisimilitude to an otherwise bald and unconvincing narrative (see how I worked Poo-Bah's words from W S Gilbert's *Mikado* in there? It has nothing whatsoever to do with gin but gives a sort of cultural gloss to my text – that's how the trick works.)

I could go on, but the question that remains is why they bother. This is a perfectly drinkable, well-made London Dry gin, sourced from the highly regarded Thames Distillers in Clapham, that offers excellent value for money. It's nicely packaged and tastes good. There is a companion Spiced Gin laced with cinnamon and nutmeg that's an exceptionally fine drop of stuff especially for cocktails such as a Negroni or a hot spiced punch as an alternative to mulled wine.

I'd be happier to see this promoted on its own merits, rather than some elaborately contrived story that really can't hold water. Wemyss have a great reputation for their single cask malt whisky; they took over the Kingsbarns craft distillery project near St Andrews and they have little or nothing to prove as third-party bottlers. So let's leave the long-dead aristos out of it.

34

DIPLÔME

BRAND OWNER: BeBo Drinks

DISTILLERY: Boudier, Dijon, France

WEBSITE: www.diplomedrygin.com

VISITOR CENTRE: No

AVAILABILITY: Specialists

OTHER VARIANTS: None

Did you know that the famous French scientist Professor Louis Pasteur started investigating the action of yeast on fermentation in a sugar-beet distillery in Lille in 1856? His work transformed the brewing and distilling industry and is the basis of everything that we know today about fermentation (basically for present purposes, turning a sugar solution into alcohol).

I mention this because the spirit base for Diplôme is made from beetroot (I assume sugar beet). That may sound odd, but in fact if something contains sugar you can ferment it, and a wide variety of sugars are found throughout nature. The yields will vary, of course, as will the flavour, but the end result will be a low-strength alcohol that can be distilled. Not many distillers today use a sugar beet base but then, as the French say, *chacun à son goût.*

I do not idly introduce this Gallic connection, for Diplôme is made in France – I note for your curiosity that neither the brand website nor the UK importers discloses the identity of the distiller, other than to say it is in Dijon. That is powerfully suggestive of Boudier, proprietors of their own Saffron gin and contract distiller of Hoxton, but, as no one will say definitively, this remains a speculation. I have no idea why they would wish to be so secretive, but there it is. I'm going to say Boudier until someone contradicts me.

What we are permitted to know is that the juniper berries, coriander, whole lemons, orange peel, angelica, saffron, iris root and fennel seed are infused in the spirit before being distilled in a pot still and eventually bottled at 44%. A fairly straightforward and old-school selection, then, with the notable exception of saffron, which again points to a circumstantial connection with Boudier. The simplicity of the recipe reflects the fact that this dates to the Second World War, when Diplôme was apparently the gin of choice of the US forces in Europe, hence the reference on the rather charming, typographically rich label (curiously similar to the Boudier house style) to the 'Original 1945 Recipe'.

Diplôme seems to have faded after the war and disappeared from the scene entirely until resurrected on the back of the current wave of enthusiasm for gins with authentic histories. It was relaunched as recently as 2013 but apparently already enjoys widespread worldwide distribution.

Beyond this, what I do not know I cannot tell. *C'est un mystère extraordinaire.*

35

DODD'S

BRAND OWNER:	The London Distillery Company Ltd
DISTILLERY:	London Distillery, Battersea, London
WEBSITE:	www.londondistillery.com
VISITOR CENTRE:	By appointment
AVAILABILITY:	Specialists
OTHER VARIANTS:	None

Poor old Ralph Dodd. This would-be entrepreneur, having failed in his dream to bore a tunnel under the River Thames, determined to start a distillery. Unfortunately, he omitted to complete the no-doubt tedious legal formalities, was challenged by rivals and in 1807 was obliged to drop his scheme without a drop ever being distilled. He died a ruined man.

You might think him more deserving of a Darwin Award than having a splendid new gin named after him. But, perverse or not, that's what the folks at Battersea's London Distillery Company (LDC) elected to do and, in his honour, they've created a splendidly packaged gin with lots of engineering references on the label – and, I'm happy to say, a very fine product to which I'm sure old Ralph would have been happy to lend his name.

The company was created to be the first distiller of whisky in London since 1903 and they have been busy making drams since, raising the funds they needed from a combination of equity financing and a clever use of crowd funding. But you have to wait for whisky, and anyway we're interested in the gin, which is available right now.

In a market now crowded by craft distillers, LDC do stand out for their obsessive approach to their product. Using their own proprietary method (though it is not dissimilar to what Hendrick's do on a much larger scale), a base spirit is distilled in Christina, their 140-litre copper pot still. The organic ingredients, which are approved by the Soil Association, include juniper, angelica, fresh lime peel, and honey from London hives. Now that's unusual, but you really can taste the difference that it makes.

A small proportion of the base is then used to macerate more delicate botanicals such as bay laurel, cardamom and red raspberry leaf for twenty-four hours. This is then distilled for a second time in 'Little Albion', a rotary evaporator (a cold vacuum still). The two spirits are married for several weeks before being hand-bottled at 47% abv and labelled at the distillery in batches of 100 to 500 bottles.

The brand's responsible drinking message (they had to have one, I suppose) is taken from Ralph Dodd's launch prospectus for his ill-fated distillery: 'It is an evil too well known to require a dissertation – for the consequence arising from bad spirits soon manifests in the destruction of its user.' And so say all of us.

36

DOROTHY PARKER

BRAND OWNER:	New York Distilling Company
DISTILLERY:	New York Distilling, Brooklyn, New York, USA
WEBSITE:	www.nydistilling.com
VISITOR CENTRE:	Yes – and the distillery tap is next door, a bar named the Shanty
AVAILABILITY:	Specialists
OTHER VARIANTS:	Perry's Tot, Chief Gowanus New Netherland Gin

'*I* like to have a Martini, two at the very most; three, I'm under the table, four I'm under my host!' Or so the legendary New York critic, poet, writer and satirist Dorothy Parker (1893–1967) is alleged to have quipped. Actually, it may merely have been attributed to her – but it is the sort of thing that she did say and it inspired New York Distilling Company to create this classic American gin.

NY Distilling is located in Brooklyn, right in the heart of New York, home to partners Allen Katz and Tom Potter, both of whom come with serious, heavyweight drinks industry credentials. By new-wave, craft distilling standards this is a substantial operation, with a 5,000-square-foot facility and a 1,000-litre Christian Carl still. Their promotional video on YouTube in which Katz walks the visitor through the story of NY Distilling shows a purposeful and well-designed set-up that's clearly capable of a significant output and some expansion in due course. There's also a great cocktail bar, the Shanty, immediately adjacent to the distillery itself.

The 44% Dorothy Parker gin is not, in fact, quite the New American gin that you might at first expect: it starts out pretty much as a classic that leads with plenty of juniper, but then reveals an unexpectedly floral twist that is surprisingly delicate. Spice then follows to suggest an underlying complexity that belies the initial sweetness. The distillery themselves say: 'Made with a fabulous blend of traditional and contemporary botanicals including hibiscus petals, this floral gin retains enough juniper bite to do Dottie, the legendary writer, poet, satirist and New Yorker, justice!'

It certainly does have some bite, but not an unpleasant one, and, though you'll likely employ this in a carefully crafted cocktail, it can be sipped neat and at room temperature with great pleasure.

With its location, impressive facilities, experienced management and cleverly positioned brands (Perry's Tot refers to the famous US Navy commander who first established trade links with Japan and Chief Gowanus was the Native American chief of the Canarsees when Brooklyn was Dutch), NY Distilling is something of a poster boy for the craft distilling community.

And now, if you'll excuse me, I have to get out of some wet clothes and into a dry Martini. (Sadly, it turns out that Dorothy didn't say that either. Shame.)

37

DURHAM

BRAND OWNER: Durham Gin Ltd

DISTILLERY: Durham Distillery, Langley Park, County Durham

WEBSITE: www.durhamdistillery.co.uk

VISITOR CENTRE: Tours by appointment only

AVAILABILITY: Limited

OTHER VARIANTS: None

Durham is the brainchild of ex-NHS chief Jon Chadwick who, following a trip to the USA where he encountered micro-distilling, was able to use his redundancy payment and other private capital to establish County Durham's first (legal) distillery. For the avoidance of doubt, this is quite separate and entirely different from the Durham Distillery in North Carolina, USA, who expect to start distilling their gin in 2015.

The North-East of England wouldn't, on first sight, be the most obvious location for a new distillery, but Durham taps into fierce local pride and a sense of identity that should provide a sound basis for future growth.

Several things make it stand out. The distillery has commissioned its own still, but not from the usual makers. Instead, the 400-litre Lily, a pot still with botanicals basket and highly traditional worm tub condenser has come from Portugal. It has a distinctly antique look, but under the guidance of Durham's Jessica Tomlinson seems to work effectively enough. Tomlinson is not only one of the very few female distillers in the country (and one of the youngest) but also one of the best qualified, holding both a Masters Degree in Chemistry and the MSc in Brewing and Distilling from Edinburgh's Heriot-Watt University.

She followed another Heriot-Watt graduate, David Wilkinson, who devised the formula for Durham but decided to return to Edinburgh to take up a post with Spencerfield Spirits (see *Edinburgh Gin,* curiously enough just over the page). No doubt we will see a gentle evolution in the taste profile of Durham gin in due course.

For the moment, what makes this small-batch operation stand out is the addition of pink peppercorns in the botanicals. It may not sound much, but the aroma really hits your nose as the spirit hits the glass. The nose is fresh, sweet and appealing; the pink peppercorns deliver that all-important pepper hit, but tempered with a soft sweetness. Durham also offers a very forward, pronounced and confident juniper aroma with undertones of orange. Two other unusual botanicals are celery seed and elderflower.

Made in batches of just 200 bottles at a time, Durham gin is still modestly priced for such handcrafted limited production. It's a confident and stylish effort from a new company.

38

EDINBURGH GIN

BRAND OWNER:	Spencerfield Spirits
DISTILLERY:	The Edinburgh Gin Distillery, 1a Rutland Place, Edinburgh
WEBSITE:	www.edinburghgindistillery.co.uk
VISITOR CENTRE:	Within Heads & Tails Bar, as distillery
AVAILABILITY:	Widespread
OTHER VARIANTS:	Raspberry, Elderflower, Rhubarb & Ginger, Cannonball (57%) and seasonal styles

Edinburgh Gin – it's made in Edinburgh in case you were wondering – could be held up as a case study for craft distilling. It's the brainchild of Jane and Alex Nicol of Spencerfield Spirits, the husband-and-wife team behind Sheep Dip and other super whiskies. But Alex is a restless sort of chap (no offence, Alex) and possessed of a fierce entrepreneurial drive.

It's said that Edinburgh once had a flourishing distilling industry producing both gin and whisky – one eighteenth-century text claims that the city was home to more than 400 illicit stills, but that owes rather more to the over-heated imagination of the partisan author (a fervent abolitionist) than any verifiable fact. Whatever the truth of the matter, gin distilling died out in Edinburgh when the Melrose-Drover Gin Distillery in Leith closed in 1974.

The Nicols re-established the tradition with a bar, visitor centre and distillery at the West end of Princes Street. Like its counterpart City of London Distillery, it's in a cosy basement, where you can see Flora and Caledonia (the stills – see diagram on p14) safely behind glass and book into some educational tours and tastings (visits from 11 a.m. to 4.30 p.m.). Being in a real bar, it's rather more fun than the light industrial units that are home to some other small batch producers. However, sales have grown so far and so fast that Edinburgh Gin isn't really 'small' any more and at least two national supermarkets now stock it.

In fact, plans are well advanced to open a considerably larger distillery on the edge of the city, close to Heriot-Watt University. Edinburgh Gin has a unique Knowledge Transfer Partnership with the UK's only university department of distilling, providing the expertise for constant experimentation with flavours and botanicals. It sounds more fun than my experience of academia, but that's what you get for reading English Lit.

A Navy strength version has recently been launched; produced in the shadow of Edinburgh Castle it's been named Cannonball. As the name would suggest, it's explosive stuff. In both expressions you'll find lots going on: a pine-led juniper note gives way to citrus, heather and spice (ginger and coriander), making them both satisfyingly complex and refreshing. Great in a classic Martini!

With Edinburgh Gin Spencerfield have lent interest, variety and colour to this most respectable and middle-class of cities: lang may their lum reek!

ELEPHANT

BRAND OWNER: Elephant Gin Ltd

DISTILLERY: Schwechower, nr Hamburg, Germany

WEBSITE: www.elephant-gin.com

VISITOR CENTRE: No

AVAILABILITY: Limited

OTHER VARIANTS: None

We all probably remember Babar from childhood; or Kipling's Elephant Child and his 'satiable curtiosity'; or tales of Jumbo (late of London Zoo) and the great showman P.T. Barnum; or Mark Twain's 'Stolen White Elephant'. These gentle giants exercise a powerful hold on our imagination. Here in the 'civilised' West we deplore the wholesale slaughter of the African elephant to satisfy the apparently insatiable Chinese demand for ivory. Though you're probably feeling vaguely bad about that, few of us (and I'm as guilty as anyone) actually do very much about it.

But now you can! It's easy! Drink Elephant Gin (no elephants harmed in the making)!

Yes, company founder Robin Gerlach and his partners were so troubled by the 35,000 African elephants killed every year that they determined to help. After something of an epiphany on an African bush holiday they hit upon the idea of making Elephant Gin and contributing 15% of its profits to elephant conservation.

Soon Gerlach had to give up his day job in finance (like Daniel Szor, another banker turned gin distiller) to concentrate on sales and marketing. Today, the product is distilled at the rather beautiful Schwechower distillery in Germany, where they make very fine fruit spirits, but the partners are actively looking to set up their own operation, probably using the current still.

I must admit to a certain cynicism, assuming that the elephants were simply a marketing gimmick. I couldn't have been more wrong: while Gerlach can and does speak eloquently about his gin he moves to a different level when talking about elephants.

You probably care more about the unusual botanicals. They include baobab, the extraordinary buchu plant, devil's claw and African wormwood, sourced with the assistance of native African tribespeople. The botanicals also include mountain pine needles, specially cut in the Salzburger Mountains to complement the juniper. It comes in a custom bottle (50cl) with a splendid closure and handsome label – one of the best-dressed craft gins you can buy.

It's not cheap but all things considered it is great value. Please don't forget that!

40

FARMER'S ORGANIC

BRAND OWNER: Chatham Imports Inc.
DISTILLERY: Undisclosed
WEBSITE: www.farmersgin.com
VISITOR CENTRE: No
AVAILABILITY: Limited
OTHER VARIANTS: None

Another small-batch gin from the United States, Farmer's has the distinction of its organic status, which it announces proudly and prominently on the label. There are a few organic gins out there, but only a few, so if this is important to you you'll have to do some searching. If you really care about such things, bear in mind that this organic certification comes from the USDA and is therefore subtly different from the UK's Soil Association. I'm not saying one is better than the other, just pointing it out.

Now, I'm not entirely convinced of the particular benefits of organic production to spirits. That's not to suggest that there aren't sound environmental and ethical reasons for organic production, it's simply a comment on the taste. But, after some consideration, that view probably comes from the dark spirits perspective, where wood maturation has a significant influence and the original spirit character is less evident. Clearly that's not the case for gin, and here – whether due to organic production or not – we have a clean, fresh and very floral-tasting gin that stands up very well against its peers.

It's helped by the 46.7% abv strength. Not overpowering but with plenty of body, this means Farmer's excels as a cocktail ingredient and is not overwhelmed by even a good slug of tonic. As an example of the 'New American Gin' style the key point in the taste is that juniper has been dialled down (compared to, say, a British classic such as Beefeater), allowing other, arguably more subtle botanicals to come to the fore.

Here we have elderflower and lemongrass that are evident on the palate, contributing to a less assertive but no less complex gin that I would expect to do well in blind tasting.

The owners, Chatham Imports, are a little coy about the distillery, simply saying that it's the same as their Crop Harvest Earth Organic vodka. Sadly, I'm none the wiser, but whoever is distilling Farmer's knows what they're about, so let's hope they keep it up.

The secret lies in the soil, you know.

41

FERDINAND'S

BRAND OWNER:	Ferdinand's
DISTILLERY:	Avadis, Wincheringen, Germany
WEBSITE:	www.saar-gin.com
VISITOR CENTRE:	No
AVAILABILITY:	Limited
OTHER VARIANTS:	Quince

There seems to be no stopping those wacky Germans trying to reinvent gin. The guys at Ferdinand's aren't happy with using thirty (thirty, count 'em) botanicals and coming up with their own individual distilling regime. Oh no. They then go and add a dollop (well, a precisely measured 2.5% by volume – they are German) of Riesling wine into the spirit prior to bottling. What's going on, you might ask, and can we really admit this as gin?

Well, it's clearly different, and, even if you'd be hard pressed to pick out all thirty botanicals (I certainly was), the initial impact is one of great power, complexity and assurance. There is an initial sweetness, presumably due to the Riesling wine, that is soon washed away by the intense botanical hit, juniper follow-through and gingery finish. It's definitely more than a gimmick or a novelty, and, having met the enthusiastic young production team I can confirm how seriously they take all this.

Most distillers will tell you that there's a realistic upper limit to the number of botanicals that you need and indeed want in your gin, the fact of the matter being that after a certain point the individual contributions get overwhelmed or even start cancelling each other out. Adding botanicals increases cost and complexity to the distilling process but doesn't necessarily increase flavour or even complexity to the taste. Different botanicals behave differently – some need to be infused in the spirit, while others perform best on a vapour tray. So working with botanicals, particularly unorthodox ones, is a tricky business and needs a confident and skilled hand to manage it well.

But distiller Andreas Vallendar comes from a long and distinguished family line of distillers that have been making fruit schnapps since 1824. His Avadis Distillery is small but expertly set up, and clearly capable of making high-quality spirit (he also makes a highly regarded Three Lander malt whisky). The Riesling wine that is added is not some supermarket plonk but from the nearby VDP Forstmeister Geltz-Zilliken vineyard, whose top vintages go into Ferdinand's gin.

When I first encountered this I was sceptical. Having tried it, however, I'm completely won over. Naturally, it's not cheap – you'll pay the equivalent of nearly £70 for a standard bottle – but this is a product you'll want to drink thoughtfully and carefully in a well-mixed cocktail.

So, to conclude: it's gin, Jim, but not as we know it. And all the better for that.

42

FILLIERS

BRAND OWNER: Graanstokerij Filliers NV,
Deinze, Belgium

DISTILLERY: Filliers, Deinze, Belgium

WEBSITE: www.filliers.be

VISITOR CENTRE: Yes

AVAILABILITY: Specialists

OTHER VARIANTS: Pine Blossom, Barrel Aged,
Tangerine (seasonal), Sloe

A family-controlled firm, Filliers were established in 1792, but started serious commercial distilling in 1880. Today they make a wide range of spirits – genever, liqueurs, advocaat, vodka, Belgian whisky and a number of excellent gins – so are both serious and well established.

The 28 Dry Gin was first created in 1928, and the name also references the twenty-eight botanicals added to juniper during distillation. So perhaps that should be 29 then, or 28½. Whatever.

Despite having been around for nearly a century, it's nothing like as well known as it should be, given its credentials and obvious quality. The reason is that Filliers' genevers and other traditional products were bigger sellers for them; gin, as we know, had faded somewhat in the last thirty years, and the UK was never a great market anyway. Hopefully that's beginning to change.

It is worth, I think, drawing your attention to the attractive apothecary's bottle with its string and label. The style has been adopted by a number of more recent gins, some of which you will find here, but this seems to be the first (certainly in recent times) to use this approach. So, it's the original and all the more credit to them: imitation is the sincerest form of flattery, they say.

Filliers don't offer much information about the botanicals, but nose and taste both suggest a high citrus content, spices, especially cardamom and coriander, candied fruits, notably orange and lemon peel. It is superbly integrated, smooth and creamy in mouthfeel; in fact, this is deceptively easy to drink neat. My regrettably small sample was finished rather quickly and I was left looking for more.

The story goes that Firmin Filliers was inspired to create this by the realisation that juniper was not only key to genever but essential to gin. In fact, trying to copy genever, but lacking the know-how, early English distillers created gin, which subsequently England made her own. In effect, Filliers worked backwards but with greater skill and knowledge than the first pioneers, and was thus able to create an enduring Belgian tribute to an archetypal English product based on a Dutch model.

Even with that complicated genesis this is a true original.

43

FORDS

BRAND OWNER: The 86 Company, New York
DISTILLERY: Thames Distillers, Timbermill
Distillery, Clapham, London
WEBSITE: www.fordsgin.com
VISITOR CENTRE: No
AVAILABILITY: Limited
OTHER VARIANTS: None

Juniper from Italy. Coriander from Romania. Orange peel from Haiti. Jasmine from China. And Indonesian cassia bark. So far, so unremarkable. But then we learn that this gin is distilled in London but reduced and bottled using water from Mendocino County in California. What's going on, you may ask. And what's the story of the very strange-looking bottle?

That's all about the bar trade, because Fords is one of the hottest things on the cocktail scene right now. The bottle was designed by and for bartenders, and is not only very easy to handle and pour but even comes with a scale embossed on the side to assist with exact measures for cocktails, and the bar's own recipes for house-made syrups. It may sound functional but bar folks love it.

The Californian water comes about thus. Fords is distilled in London by Thames Distillers' very own Charles Maxwell (whom you will meet time and again in these pages as he is something of an *éminence grise* in the gin world) but then shipped at high strength to the Charbay Distillery in the Napa Valley where it is reduced to a bottling strength of 45%. Apparently this reduces the carbon footprint. They don't mention shipping the bottles back to the UK though. Strange, that.

It may have been created by and for bar people, but that doesn't mean you can't have it at home. The smarter UK specialists have seen how strongly this is trending and you can pick up a bottle for under £30, which is very fair value. Just having a bottle will impress your more knowledgeable friends and enhance your credentials as a gin connoisseur. Surely, bragging rights like that are worth thirty quid?

As you'd expect, given this history, this is a gin just dying to jump into a cocktail. So, both the taste and aromas are quite pronounced: not assertive, aggressive or unpleasant but very definite and quite capable of holding their own in a mixed drink after dilution. There are just nine botanicals, so this is not an overly complicated recipe, but the end product is complex, well integrated and consistent in flavour delivery from aroma to finish. Look for aromatic floral and citrus notes on the nose, with an evolution into juniper and drying spices.

Bar people know, you know, and this is the proof of the pudding. Expect to see more of Fords in a bar near you, because this is going to catch on fast (if it hasn't already).

44

FOUR PILLARS

BRAND OWNER:	Healesville Distilling Company Pty Ltd
DISTILLERY:	Four Pillars, South Warrandyte, Victoria, Australia
WEBSITE:	www.fourpillarsgin.com
VISITOR CENTRE:	By arrangement
AVAILABILITY:	Specialists
OTHER VARIANTS:	Barrel Aged, Gunpowder Proof

As you probably know, the Australians make some great wines in the Yarra. I can still recall a bottle of Yarra Yering Dry Red Wine No. 2 (prosaic title, stunning wine) that has me licking my lips at the memory. So I jump to the assumption that they can probably manage to get something drinkable out of a still.

There is a vibrant craft industry producing whisky, mainly in Tasmania, that has surprised a few folks, and some jolly decent gins are to be found down under as well. One of the newest but most exciting is Four Pillars, also located in the Yarra Valley, not so very far away from Melbourne where the rival Melbourne Gin Company have based their operations. But there appears to be plenty of domestic support, and with growing international interest in these craft gins there is no reason why they can't both prosper.

Four Pillars ran a highly successful crowd-funding campaign that meant their first release sold out before it was made. An impressive £15,500 was raised – quite something for a product that at that point didn't exist and evidence of enthusiastic local backing that gives the brand a vocal and financially committed supporter base. However, they are far from limited in their horizons and ambitions, with a stated aim 'to make the best craft spirits in Australia'. That is already a demanding goal and will only get harder. So what are they all about?

The heart of the operation is the first new Christian Carl still in Australia, which they named Wilma, after head distiller Cameron Mackenzie's late mother. Mackenzie comes from a wine background, believes strongly in the use of fresh fruit (he's not alone in this, but it is unusual) and having taken close to eighteen months to come up with the final gin is using some unorthodox botanicals such as lemon myrtle and Tasmanian pepper berry leaf. He also posts an amusing blog on the distillery's website.

Looking into the distillery more closely, I was reminded of The Macallan single malt whisky and their 'six pillars'. Guess how many Four Pillars work with? That's right, just four. One, their copper pot still. Two, the triple-filtered Yarra Valley water. Three, the botanicals: added to the pepperberry, lemon myrtle and fresh oranges we find cinnamon, cardamom, coriander seeds, lavender and star anise and the classic juniper and angelica root. Four, the distillers love what they do and love what they have made. Fair dinkum, mate!

GENIUS

BRAND OWNER: Genius Liquids LLC

DISTILLERY: Genius, Austin, Texas, USA

WEBSITE: www.geniusliquids.com

VISITOR CENTRE: No

AVAILABILITY: Limited – currently USA only

OTHER VARIANTS: Navy Strength

It takes a certain amount of brazen confidence, not to say chutzpah, to label yourself, your distillery and your gin as Genius, especially when the company is brand new and the gin only launched in June 2013. Presumably they thought about calling themselves Novice or Cadet, then knocked back a couple of large ones and thought they might as well save all that boring apprentice and learning stuff and just go straight to the bull's-eye. They are from Texas, after all.

Actually, the Lone Star state, formerly an independent republic, is rapidly developing as a centre of craft distilling and, without degenerating too far into predictable and clichéd stereotypes, does seem to be a hotbed of entrepreneurial initiative and inventive boutique distillers. So for partners Mike Groener and Charles Cheung this was fertile territory.

They describe their process as 'hot and cold'. By that they mean that, after making their own base spirit using a six-plate copper still, they infuse this at room temperature with the first half (the Cold) of their botanical blend for over seventy-two hours (this blend includes elderflower, lavender, lime peel, angelica root and some undisclosed others). When ready, this is distilled again (the Hot) in a process that pushes vapours through the remaining ingredients enclosed in a basket within the still. These heat-activated ingredients include juniper, cardamom, coriander and a few others that again they keep secret. Each 'Hot' preparation involves the toasting and muddling of all the fresh ingredients.

The result is in the 'new Western' style, in that the juniper note is very much in the background, but I would hesitate to classify it under that label as the initial taste is quite hot and spicy, with the cardamom to the fore but fleeting hints of washed samphire. Going back to the base spirit, the interesting thing is that Genius have gone to the trouble of making this themselves, rather than buying in neutral grain spirit as so many distillers do.

Rather eccentrically, however, they've used sugar as the base ingredient. That may explain the somewhat offbeat initial impact, and it certainly distinguishes this newcomer as out of the ordinary. The flavours seem to me to work best in a cocktail and will appeal to the adventurous and experimental drinker looking for something different.

GERANIUM

BRAND OWNER: Hammer & Son, Fredericksberg, Denmark

DISTILLERY: The Langley Distillery, Langley Green, Warley, West Midlands

WEBSITE: www.geraniumgin.com

VISITOR CENTRE: No

AVAILABILITY: Limited

OTHER VARIANTS: None

Geranium was developed in Denmark by father and son team Hudi and Henrik Hammer, though unfortunately Hudi died before he could see this fascinating product launched in September 2009. It arrived in the UK the following year, but, as it is actually distilled here, there is a sense of it coming home (saves all that Viking pillaging, not to mention the other thing).

If it sounds a little gimmicky, well, actually it isn't. In fact, Henrik Hammer is a long-standing IWSC judge where he is described as 'an enthusiastic ginologist, entrepreneur, distiller, brand owner, judge, lecturer, cocktalian, imbiber with the overall objective to educate people within gin and to extend the knowledge about gin.'

And how better to do that than to create your own gin based on some serious science? Henrik's father had a background as a chemist in the perfume industry, and together they began to explore the possible contribution of the geranium plant to gin. Geranium, they discovered, was historically renowned for its therapeutic properties, being used to treat depression amongst other things, along with juniper, coriander and lemon. They, of course, are vital ingredients in gin.

Together they began analysing and distilling geranium leaves, albeit on a domestic scale, to extract geraniol formate, rose oxide and citronelol. The significance of their discovery was that very similar compounds are already found in the fruits, berries and spices used for classic cocktails. Hence they concluded that geranium was both a legitimate constituent for gin and likely to work with the other botanicals, heightening and enhancing their flavours.

Having developed the concept at a test-kitchen level they turned to Langley's to help them take production to a commercial scale. The product found ready acceptance and has won a number of awards and recommendations, thus confirming Henrik Hammer's theories. It is bottled at 44%, having started life as 100% wheat-based spirit in Langley's copper pot still Constance. The other botanicals comprise juniper, lemon, orange, coriander, cassia, orris, angelica and liquorice.

As you might expect, it's a crisp and floral gin with a slightly sweet note but without losing the essential element of juniper. A triumph for flower power, you might say.

47

GILBEY'S

BRAND OWNER: Diageo

DISTILLERY: BeamSuntory, USA.

WEBSITE: www.beamsuntory.com
/brands/gilbeys

VISITOR CENTRE: No

AVAILABILITY: Limited (in UK, widespread
in USA)

OTHER VARIANTS: None

How are the mighty fallen! Tell it not in London, publish it not in the streets of Camden, lest the vodka drinkers rejoice …

I can recall Gilbey's from my early drinking years, largely I will now admit because I liked the bottle and label (it has evolved slightly over the years). But today Gilbey's, once a colossus that bestrode the world of drinks, is reduced to a pale 37.5% imitation of its former self and produced only in the USA under licence from the brand owner Diageo, who elected some years ago to concentrate their efforts on Gordon's and Tanqueray. Gilbey's, once the largest wine and spirits company in the UK but slowly subsumed in (by turn) Watney Mann, Grand Metropolitan and eventually Diageo, was condemned to a sad decline.

There were some interesting bumps in the road. In July 1971 they ran print advertising in the USA under the headline 'Break out the frosty bottle', held by connoisseurs of such matters to be 'a classic design of subliminal art'. Apparently, if you look at it long enough the word 'sex' appears in the ice cubes and various other explicitly erotic images can be detected. Keep looking.

The late, great Terry Thomas (English comic actor, look him up) appeared in TV advertising for the brand, but surely their greatest moment was the 1982 print campaign by the artist and cartoonist Glen Baxter. Baxter's surreal vision expresses the essential Englishness of gin, his characters exhibiting great sangfroid and maintaining a stiff upper lip in the most bizarre and improbable of situations while sustained by a refreshing Gilbey's and tonic. Perhaps, on reflection, that's why I loved the brand. No one else seems to have done: the campaign lasted barely a year.

Founded in 1857 by Walter and Alfred Gilbey on their return from the Crimean War the firm was a tremendous success, eventually owning top Bordeaux chateaux, several single malts and a huge gin distillery in Camden (see entry for Half Hitch gin). By 1920 they were distilling in Australia and Canada, and in 1938 in the USA. Walter Gilbey was a prolific author, writing mainly on various aspects of the horse. His pamphlet *Notes on Alcohol* is exceptionally rare but contains a most interesting defence of direct-fired distilling so far as it relates to whisky.

The family connection ceased in 1972 with the sale to Watney Mann. Sadly, I haven't drunk it in years: *sic transit gloria mundi*.

48

GIN MARE

BRAND OWNER: Giró Ribot & Global Premium
Brands, SA

DISTILLERY: Destilerías Miquel Guansé,
Vilanova i la Geltrú, Spain

WEBSITE: www.ginmare.com

VISITOR CENTRE: No

AVAILABILITY: Specialists

OTHER VARIANTS: None

Mundus appellatur caelum, terra et mare', the Latin for 'the world is called heaven, earth and sea' (possibly a reference to the work of the seventh-century saint Isidore, Archbishop of Seville, whose collection of ancient texts greatly influenced the late medieval church) is to be found on a stained-glass window in a former chapel in the little seaside town of Vilanova i la Geltrú on Spain's Costa Gourada. So what, you may ask.

It also appears on the rather striking bottle of Gin Mare – Sea Gin – which today is made in said former chapel. Imagine, a chapel dedicated to gin with the still placed dramatically where the altar once stood: truly they take their gin with an almost religious devotion in Spain.

Since its launch in 2008 Gin Mare, soaked in all the influences of its Mediterranean home has proved highly successful on the cocktail scene, though when partnered with its stablemate 1724 tonic, it also makes a stunning G&T – especially when served in the generous Spanish style. It is the creation of Marc and Manuel Giró, the fourth generation of a noted Spanish distilling house that is behind the popular GinMG and other brands. Their goal was to create a new contemporary, premium gin that reflected its origins.

To develop it, they exhaustively tested forty-five different botanicals, finally settling on a range that, along with wild juniper harvested from the family estate, included Arbequina olives (small, low yielding and expensive), sweet and bitter oranges and lemons (all painstakingly hand-peeled), rosemary, thyme and basil, and more commonly seen gin botanicals such as coriander and cardamom. Hard though it is to credit, the fruit zests are macerated in neutral spirit for fully twelve months before it is deemed ready for distillation to begin.

That takes place in the distillery's custom-designed 250-litre Florentine pot still (interestingly a similar design is used in perfume manufacture and at G'Vine), after which the finished product is bottled, literally next door to the distillery, at 42.7%.

As might be expected from the unorthodox use of olives, rosemary and so on, this is a different-tasting gin – and one that once tasted won't be forgotten. Understandably, it's not the cheapest gin on the market but, with its unusual make-up and distinctive presentation, still offers excellent value.

If this is the sea, don't hesitate to dive right in.

49

GORDON'S ORIGINAL SPECIAL DRY

BRAND OWNER:	Diageo plc
DISTILLERY:	Cameronbridge, Fife
WEBSITE:	www.gordons-gin.co.uk
VISITOR CENTRE:	No
AVAILABILITY:	Universal
OTHER VARIANTS:	Also available in Cucumber, Elderflower and Sloe styles, and as Original London Dry (47.3% abv)

If you don't ask for the gin you really want, this is the gin you'll probably get. It really is everywhere. I suppose if you add enough ice and tonic of your choice there's nothing at all wrong with it – indeed traditionalists will enjoy the strong juniper influence – but there's not that much to get terribly excited about, either.

Frankly, this was how gin lost its way, became dull, staid and boring, and surrendered to vodka and light rum. When in 1992 the UK version was reduced to 37.5% abv you really did feel they had run up the white flag, chucked in the towel and given up the ghost. In fairness, the Original London Dry version (mainly duty-free shops) is a healthier 47.3% abv, which makes all the difference, but for the classic London gin to drop to the level of an anaemic supermarket own-label really was disappointing. Gordon's may as well have told us to BOGOF.

After nearly 225 years of history I imagine that founder Alexander Gordon was less than impressed that some bean-counter determined the future of his creation, a global English icon if ever there was one, to be a corporate cash cow. Because, make no mistake, less than twenty-five years ago the prevailing industry view was that gin was finished and it was only a matter of time before it joined shrub, malmsey and other forgotten old favourites in the great off-licence in the sky.

Slowly but surely, most of the distinctive Gordon's variants – Old Tom, Orange and Lemon gins – were killed off, and though their Sloe gin staggered on it was hard to find. But it's amazing what a bit of competition can do: enter Bombay Sapphire and, a little later, Hendrick's from William Grant & Sons. From a standing start these two ripped up the rulebook: gin wasn't fuddy-duddy, in decline and only to be sold on price. With clever marketing and great products, they proved that you could sell a premium gin to younger drinkers with a funky image – and, what was important, lots and lots of it.

Hendrick's in particular rethought what gin meant and, though they might not see it quite this way, the Gordon's people have a lot to thank them for. Now we can enjoy Gordon's Crisp Cucumber (whatever gave them that idea?) and the subtly sweet Elderflower.

Time for an Old Tom revival? We wait breathlessly.

50

GRANIT

BRAND OWNER: Alte Hausbrennerei Penninger GmbH
DISTILLERY: Alte Hausbrennerei Penninger, Hauzenberg, Bavaria, Germany
WEBSITE: www.granit-gin.com
VISITOR CENTRE: Schnapps Museum
AVAILABILITY: Specialists
OTHER VARIANTS: None

Here's a little-known gin from Bavaria — well, I'll admit that I knew nothing at all about it until I was judging the 2015 World Gin Awards. What happens at this particular stage is that judges are sent lots of little sample bottles labelled only with a code number and the strength, a scoring sheet with the code, and instructions. I faithfully worked my way through a large box of gins — some good, some not so great — and duly scored them.

Some time later my curiosity could not be contained, and when all the scores were in and counted I asked the organisers to identify the one gin that I had scored the highest. And here it was, and to my frustration I knew nothing at all about it, except that I obviously liked it very much (at the time of writing we don't know if my fellow judges agreed).

I described it thus: 'Very attractive nose. Clove, vanilla, nutmeg and pine-y juniper. Well balanced and complex.' They don't give you much room for comments, but this was high praise. So, once I had the identity, I had to check this out.

It's made by the old-established family firm of Penninger who describe themselves as the leading distiller of traditional Bavarian speciality spirits. Granit is a relatively new product, the creation of Stefan Penninger, the latest generation of the family. He has chosen native Bavarian forest plants combined with a highly unusual maturation process. Granit's twenty-eight botanicals include classics such as lemon, coriander and cardamom combined with the local melissa, bald-money (similar to lovage) and gentian root.

Once distilled, the gin is matured for several months in earthenware vats before being filtered through locally hand-cut granite stones of varying sizes using the so-called 'Oxy-Esterator', a fifty-year-old technology which had pride of place in their Penninger Bavarian Schnapps Museum. Hence the name Granit and hence the small granite stone attached to the bottle. This can be placed in the freezer and then used as an ice cube to prevent your drink from becoming watered down. It's also, according to the distillery at least, guaranteed to be a conversation starter! Bottled at 42%, Granit is claimed to be 100% organic.

Now you know as much as I do, so let's hope supplies find their way here soon.

51

GREENALL'S ORIGINAL

BRAND OWNER: Quintessential Brands

DISTILLERY: G & J Distillers, Warrington

WEBSITE: www.greenallsgin.com

VISITOR CENTRE: No

AVAILABILITY: Universal

OTHER VARIANTS: None

If you wait a bit you may find Greenall's Original on offer for £12 a bottle. I did, without even looking particularly hard. Frankly, that's quite the bargain for a gin produced in Britain's longest-established gin distillery.

Of course, much has changed since 1761. The founder, one Thomas Dakin, leased his business to Greenall's the brewers who took full control in 1870. The company survived a huge fire in 2005 but the family sold to Quintessential Brands the following year. Perhaps coincidentally the distillery then appointed its first ever female master distiller Joanne Moore, only the seventh in the distillery's history. With a substantial own-label business the company claims to be responsible for the production of some 60% of the gin sold in the UK and around 20% of quality gin produced worldwide.

So you'd expect a bottle carrying the Greenall name to be quite a respectable drop of Vera Lynn and this does not disappoint (hence my surprise at the bargain price). Despite being bottled at 37.5% abv, which has something to do with that, of course, it's a good, solid stand-by that could easily pass for something more expensive.

Another contributor to the price is the simple closure; known to the trade as a ROPP (Roll-On Pilfer Proof) or humble screw cap. This is obviously considerably cheaper than the cork stoppers adopted, largely for marketing reasons, by more expensive brands and – this is the important bit – *better*.

That's because a percentage of all the cork produced – whatever the cork producers maintain – is subject to cork taint, from a contaminant known as TCA. That stands for 2,4,6-trichloroanisole, the chemical responsible for 'corked' wine; the dreaded musty aroma of wet cardboard that leaps instantly from an affected bottle. It affects spirits too, but where in a strongly flavoured whisky it may not be apparent other than at high concentrations, in something more delicate such as gin it will result in a spoiled bottle. The distillers take the risk because marketing tells them that a cork closure is essential to a premium image. (Synthetic cork is OK; just watch out for the real thing.)

So don't be ashamed if your bottle has a screw cap; it protects the flavour and, in a case like this, delivers a good old-fashioned, no-nonsense gin that's a lot better than the price would suggest.

GREENBRIER

BRAND OWNER: Smooth Ambler Spirits

DISTILLERY: Smooth Ambler, Lewisburg,
Greenbrier Valley, West Virginia,
USA

WEBSITE: www.smoothambler.com

VISITOR CENTRE: Yes

AVAILABILITY: Specialists

OTHER VARIANTS: Barrel Aged

Smooth Ambler is another of the burgeoning small craft distillers that add such colour and variety to the American distilling scene – but fortunately they feel able to spare UK drinkers just a few of the 7,500 or so bottles that they make each year.

Located in Greenbrier County, West Virginia, they are very much in the artisanal Appalachian distilling tradition with its Scots-Irish roots. As you would expect, they make several whiskeys but, like many small US distilleries, they also distil white spirits.

This is no longer a case of some good ol' boys turning out a few barrels of white lightning, but a small and technically advanced distillery. They like to do things the right way, and this grain-to-glass, small-batch gin is no exception. The base spirit (the distillery's own Whitewater vodka) is made from 68% corn (grown on a single farm based within half an hour of the distillery), 16% wheat and 16% malted barley. The botanicals, which are quadruple distilled using a hybrid pot and column still, are juniper, orange peel, lemon peel, cardamom, coriander, angelica root and black pepper.

Very much a 'Western' or Americanised gin, it has a round mouthfeel with citrus and spicy notes and while delivering juniper, backs off compared to a typical London Dry. It's warm, nutty and welcoming on the nose with a clear citrus influence. Independent judges seem to like it: it was rated 91/100 by American Craft Spirits and awarded 94 points by *Wine Enthusiast* magazine.

All in all, it's an impressive debut from a distillery that was only established in 2009. Joint founders TAG Galyean and John Little (also the head distiller) head the small team. Production is labour intensive, but when it comes to bottling, friends, family and members of the local community are invited in to lend a hand with each bottle being hand signed by whoever bottled it – this could be a director, an uncle or the lady from the store down the road.

The distillery welcomes visitors with free tastings on weekday afternoons and free tours on Fridays and Saturdays. Walk-up visitors are accommodated wherever possible but phone in advance to be sure. And, if you really love the place, you can even hire the distillery for a party which surely has to beat distilling moonshine in the woods!

53

G'VINE FLORAISON

BRAND OWNER:	EWG Spirits & Wine, Cognac, France
DISTILLERY:	S.A.S. EuroWineGate, Villevert, Merpins, France
WEBSITE:	www.escapetothegrape.com or www.g-vine.com
VISITOR CENTRE:	No
AVAILABILITY:	Specialists
OTHER VARIANTS:	Nouaison

G'Vine would like you to know five things about their gin.

First, it's made in France from grape spirit. Second and uniquely, it uses the grape flower as a botanical. Third, there are two styles: the lighter Floraison (40%) and the more traditional Nouaison (43.9%). Fourth, they make it in the Charente region of Cognac. That feels more like a refinement of number one, but we'll let them off. And, finally, it's distilled by Jean-Sébastien Robicquet, who created it back in 2005. Well, someone has to make it, so I think they're padding the list here: let's call it three things.

But G'Vine is no longer the only gin distilled using a grape-based spirit (Madrid's 'urban distillery' Santamanía does this; so does Chilgrove in Chichester as well as the Menorcan Xoriguer). However it was almost certainly the first new wave gin to do this, and it is genuinely unusual to find gin made in Cognac (though Citadelle are also there, using a more conventional wheat spirit).

Floraison is the more unusual and experimental of the two, more delicate and showing more of the influence of the grape flowers. Using them as a botanical really does seem to be unique, and presents unique challenges: for one thing, there is only a window of around a fortnight in which they can be picked before they become small grapes, which is what Nature had planned for them all along.

After studying oenology, and then training as a lawyer, Jean-Sébastien worked in the international cognac trade before returning to the family vineyards. So he brought the sensitivity of a trained winemaker to white spirits, observing that vodka and gin were growing far more rapidly than cognac and that their consumers were more open to innovation than the more traditionally orientated brandy drinker. It also didn't hurt that while cognac takes years to reach maturation, white spirits are ready much, much faster.

And so G'Vine was born. If you're not a very traditionally minded gin drinker you will probably prefer Floraison, whereas Nouaison will appeal more to the hard-core aficionado. The spicier, fuller flavour is influenced by a different balance of botanicals bringing the classic juniper and citrus notes to the fore.

Floraison by contrast, may just be the gin to persuade vodka drinkers to try a grown-up drink. (Sorry, vodka drinkers, but you deserve it!)

54

HALF HITCH

BRAND OWNER: Holdsworth Spirits & Company
DISTILLERY: Half Hitch, Camden Lock, London
WEBSITE: www.halfhitch.london
VISITOR CENTRE: Under development
AVAILABILITY: Specialists
OTHER VARIANTS: None

My first thought was, what a great-looking bottle and label! But the founder of Half Hitch gin previously worked in marketing for global drinks giant Bacardi and the design reflects the professionalism you would expect from that background. The designers have worked with the Half Hitch knot – a round turn and two half hitches as if you cared – used to moor barges on nearby Camden Lock. Whether you know that or not, it is still a rather handsome presentation with, it occurs to me, a slight masculine bias.

Like several other small distillers, founder Mark Holdsworth has gone down the small-batch route using a rota-vap, but adopted a slightly different approach. His foundation is a gin prepared by Langley's (with angelica root, cassia bark, coriander seed, juniper, liquorice root, sweet lemon, orange peel and orris root), but he then adds his own cold distillate of hay along with black tea, bergamot, wood and pepper tinctures made in Camden Lock. The result is a unique and bespoke blend. Tea occurs in Beefeater's premium 24 brand and Spain's Sikkim but otherwise is a pretty unusual botanical, hence Holdsworth's clever social media hashtag #theGwithTea.

Half Hitch's core flavour comes from Malawian black tea (reblended each season for optimum flavour and consistency) and Calabrian bergamot. The bergamot, a natural cross between a bitter orange and a lemon, provides the all-important citrus boost that many of us love in our gins, especially if destined for the cocktail glass.

Camden was once home to W&A Gilbey's huge gin distilling and warehousing operations, with a massive 800,000-gallon warehouse. An express train exported gin around the world, but only ghosts and shadows now remain, hinted at in street names such as Juniper Crescent. But in their day, Gilbey were gin royalty, and it is today's royal family that has given Half Hitch an early boost with an invitation by HRH Duke of York to one of his Pitch@Palace events. As Mark Holdsworth recounts it: 'With an audience of Britain's leading business leaders, this has quickly led to some fantastic introductions and allowed me to bring my premium gin to influential bar industry figures ... I have been taken aback by the resulting speed of listings in London's premier bars and restaurants.' No hitch there, then.

55

HAYMAN'S OLD TOM

BRAND OWNER: Hayman Ltd

DISTILLERY: Haymans, Witham, Essex

WEBSITE: www.hayman-distillers.co.uk
and www.haymansgin.com

VISITOR CENTRE: No

AVAILABILITY: Widespread

OTHER VARIANTS: London Dry, 1850 Reserve,
Sloe, 1820 Liqueur, Royal Dock

One could in all honesty devote an entire book to Hayman Distillers. Stand aside, newcomers, for here we have the fifth generation of a family of gin distillers – gin aristocracy if you will.

Their story starts in 1863 when the current chairman Christopher Hayman's great-grandfather James Burrough purchased a London gin rectifying business – their most famous brand, of course, then and now was Beefeater. Christopher joined that company in 1969 and was responsible for the distillation and production of Beefeater until 1987 when it was sold to Whitbread, then a brewery company (how things change – they stopped brewing in 2001 and today own Premier Inn and Costa Coffee).

But Whitbread and distilling didn't really get on and a mere two years later they had sold all their whisky and gin operations, though Hayman successfully bought back the Fine Alcohols Division (the part of the business that eventually became today's Hayman Distillers) and was also a part owner of Thames Distillers. Burroughs ended up owned by Pernod Ricard – sorry, it's hard to keep up with this stuff, but it is important.

Thames Distillers subsequently produced the Hayman's brands, beginning in 2004 with the launch of the 1820 Gin Liqueur – all of the varying expressions follow original family recipes, using just ten core botanicals, albeit in different proportions.

Today, the Haymans are distilling again at Witham in Essex in 'Marjorie', a dedicated copper pot still of 450-litres capacity, handmade by the German family company Carl who began making stills just six years after James Burrough opened his business (then in all likelihood using a London-made John Dore still). That was installed as recently as June 2013.

Old Tom, having been discontinued at some time in the 1950s, was relaunched in November 2007, following demand from the leading edge of London cocktail mixologists who were seeking to recreate classic recipes from Victorian and Edwardian books. It's considered the standard bearer for the category, with a subtle sweetness derived as much from liquorice as the added sugar.

If Haymans had done nothing else than bring back the Old Tom style from the great gin palace in the sky they would still be greatly respected . . . but read on.

HAYMAN'S 1820 LIQUEUR

BRAND OWNER: Hayman Ltd
DISTILLERY: Haymans, Witham, Essex
WEBSITE: www.hayman-distillers.co.uk
and www.haymansgin.com
VISITOR CENTRE: No
AVAILABILITY: Widespread
OTHER VARIANTS: London Dry, 1850 Reserve,
Sloe, Old Tom, Royal Dock

Welcome back! The Hayman's story continues with this, the world's first gin liqueur.

The 1820 date refers not as you might expect to some faded old recipe kept in a vault somewhere but to the date that the original distillery purchased by James Burrough was originally founded. So it's a fairly tenuous link, but I think they may be forgiven as this in all probability does give us some idea of what gin *may* have tasted like 200 years ago. Of course, the base spirit employed here is a great deal higher quality than the products on offer way back then, when the sugar was added to disguise the hastily distilled and probably poor quality gin being used. In fact, there was an alarmingly high probability that it had been adulterated with oil of turpentine (if you were lucky) or sulphuric acid (if you weren't).

So gin has moved on, and we should all be glad of it. And the quest for authenticity would seem to have its limits, if only in respect of our health and safety. But the idea of a gin liqueur is a worthwhile one, and all credit to Haymans for bringing us this expression which replicates something which might have been: an interesting philosophical proposition if you consider that for a moment.

The 1820 liqueur has proved particularly popular in Spain apparently, where it is served simply with tonic though it works equally well in those cocktails that employ a dash of syrup. As noted previously, Haymans adopt a straightforward, deliberately retro approach to botanicals, eschewing the more arcane and perversely obscure ingredients that, in their search for novelty, some new wave gins have embraced. In fact, they use the same ten in all of their gins: it's only the proportions that vary.

In this case, while the sugar is evident in the taste and mouthfeel, there is also a pleasant citrus balance and some evidence of spices; juniper makes a late entry on the palate. All in all it's a pleasing addition to the drinking repertoire that comes with impeccable distilling credentials and an enviable provenance.

Also from Haymans you may find a classic London Dry, the Navy Strength Royal Dock and their 1850 Reserve, this last being rested for around a month in casks formerly used to mature Scotch whisky, the aim being to recreate the conditions under which gin would have been stored and transported in the middle of the nineteenth century.

HENDRICK'S

BRAND OWNER: William Grant & Sons

DISTILLERY: Girvan, Ayrshire

WEBSITE: www.hendricksgin.com

VISITOR CENTRE: No

AVAILABILITY: Universal

OTHER VARIANTS: A very limited run of Hendrick's Kanaracuni was created (largely for private tasting events) in 2013.

Hard though it is to believe, Hendrick's has only been with us since 1999, and wasn't launched in the UK until 2003, but the apothecary-style bottle and ingenious *faux*-Victorian marketing are powerfully suggestive of something a great deal older.

As the website and promotional material are at great pains to insist, this is a quite unusual product. But this is entirely in character for the owners, William Grant & Sons, who remain family-owned and determinedly independent. Whisky drinkers will know them as the proprietors of Glenfiddich single malt (and several other fine whiskies). Since 1887, the company has followed its own path. Hendrick's is no exception: perhaps only Grants would have named a brand after a senior family member's gardener, though it is said he tended the roses that inspired its distinctive taste.

The distilling process (sadly, closed to the public) is quite unusual: Hendrick's use a blend of spirits produced from a 1948 Carterhead still, and a vintage pot still dating to 1860. Both were bought at auction in 1966 by the late Charles Grant Gordon, who built the original Girvan distillery. He appears to have purchased them on a whim, but they were restored to working order and produce strikingly different styles of spirit due to their different construction and methods of distillation. The two spirits are blended together, and essences of Bulgarian rose petals and cucumber added (they are too delicate a flavour to be distilled with the other botanicals).

The brand was something of a sensation and, with Bombay Sapphire, may be credited with transforming the market. It has certainly been responsible for unleashing a range of less orthodox flavours on an unsuspecting world. This may well be deplored by purists but there is no denying its immensely powerful influence in inspiring a new generation of boutique distillers.

I'm personally quite conflicted about Hendrick's. I applaud their huge contribution to the category; I have the greatest of respect for their astute marketing; I recognise that it's a very well-made product from a highly respected company but I simply don't like the taste – which moves too far from traditional juniper-led gin for my palate. I think of it as a gin for people who don't particularly like gin.

You may well love it, however, so don't let me put you off.

HERNÖ

BRAND OWNER: Hernö Brenneri AB
DISTILLERY: Hernö, Dala, Ångermanland, Sweden
WEBSITE: www.hernogin.com
VISITOR CENTRE: Yes
AVAILABILITY: Specialists
OTHER VARIANTS: Navy Strength, Juniper Cask, Old Tom, Blackcurrant (limited edition)

This is a 'Swedish gin miracle', apparently. Big claim, but in a few short years Hernö have been busy collecting an impressive number of awards. The company was founded by Jon Hillgren who had worked in London as a bartender. There he discovered gin (it wasn't lost, it's just that he didn't know much about it until then). Much experimentation and many trials later, Jon founded Hernö Gin Distillery in 2011, which proudly claims to be Sweden's first dedicated gin distillery and the world's northernmost (as we go to print, but on current trends it won't be long before someone starts distilling at the North Pole).

The distillery, built to resemble a traditional Swedish red-and-white painted wooden manor house, is home to Kierstin, a 250-litre Carl copper still, first installed on 29 May 2012 – I quote the entire date just to demonstrate the comparative youth of this operation.

I'm not entirely surprised that it does well in competitions, where more forceful and strongly flavoured products can stand out in an extended tasting. The 'Swedish Excellence' standard product is certainly an assertive, hot and spicy liquid, which initially drinks stronger than its 40.5% abv. I can see how it might cut through jaded palates but, interestingly, while the majority of its really big medals have come from a trade magazine competition Hernö's Swedish Excellence hasn't got past bronze medal level with either the International Spirits Competition or the International Wine and Spirits Competition. That's not to disparage what has been achieved, but most independent observers would look to the ISC and IWSC panels as being among the more demanding on the competition circuit. Certainly they have very experienced judges and a rigorous tasting procedure. Still, it's early days, and, as they say, God loves a trier.

And, if you like bold flavours you may well care for this. I think Jon Hillgren deserves a great deal of credit for creating a product that stands out from the mainstream and can generate an enthusiastic following of supporters. His other products, especially the Juniper Cask style are highly innovative and well worth exploring. Rumour is that Hernö may release a sampling pack of four 20cl bottles of their different styles – that would make for a memorable vertical tasting and certainly goes straight onto my birthday list.

And shortly, via Hoxton, we'll return to Sweden.

59

HOXTON

BRAND OWNER: Calabrese Harte Enterprises

DISTILLERY: Boudier, Dijon, France

WEBSITE: www.hoxtongin.com

VISITOR CENTRE: No

AVAILABILITY: Specialists

OTHER VARIANTS: None (probably just as well – read on)

Researching Hoxton gin on the web (as one does), it's not very long before you come across a slew of hostile comments. The influential Simon Difford highlighted it on his website's 'Page of Shame' (not, I can tell you, where the PR wanted it to appear). But in a review uncannily reminiscent of those classic 'Disgusted of Tunbridge Wells' letters, my all-time favourite had to be this cutting assessment on The Cocktail Geek's blog.

Rating it one star ('Terrible. Only drink for a dare.') the conclusion could scarcely have been more damning: 'Hoxton gin is quite frankly the most disappointing spirit I have yet to taste. The flavour profile is not only offensive to the senses, but it strays so far away from what a gin is intended to be that it really should not be considered as such. A spectacular failure.'

Ouch!

Now, to be fair, the bottle does carry the words 'Warning! Grapefruit and Coconut' in very large letters right on the front, so there shouldn't be any confusion about what's in there. Yes, as far as I'm concerned, it somewhat resembles what I would imagine a Malibu and Lilt cocktail to taste like (not that I would ever drink such a thing). It's certainly not gin.

And that's where the problem lies. Gin is *supposed* to be led by juniper, that's the point. In fact, that's the law. So for Hoxton to label itself gin, and argue as it does that it is aimed at 'youthful trendy cats', is disingenuous in the extreme. Be honest, call this a 'Spirit Drink' and move on. To suggest, as they do on their ghastly website, that this is 'the most distinctive gin in the world' is palpably absurd.

Hoxton – the place and the gin – needs to get over itself. By the time ancient old fogies such as me have registered that Hoxton is supposed to be edgy, hip and trendy, the real cutting-edge creatives have been priced out by bankers and hedge fund traders, just desperate to absorb some contemporary culture and hang out with the cool kids – who live in Stoke Newington now apparently (wrote Buxton, in a pathetic attempt to establish just how right-on and happening he really is).

I think we should move on. As you can probably gather, not being a youthful trendy cat, I didn't really care for this.

HVEN

BRAND OWNER: Backafallsbyn AB

DISTILLERY: Backafallsbyn, Hven, Sweden

WEBSITE: www.hven.com

VISITOR CENTRE: Yes

AVAILABILITY: Specialists

OTHER VARIANTS: None

Pay attention, for this is going to get complex. Established in 2008 to create Swedish whisky, the Backafallsbyn distillery is Sweden's third-ever pot still distillery, part of a wider movement there to create artisanal spirits in what was traditionally a heavily regulated market, with stringent government controls. It's located on the tiny island of Hven, situated in Öresund, between Denmark and Sweden, which you can only reach by boat. With fewer than 350 inhabitants, think more of Jura than Islay.

So far, so simple. But wait. Oak aged gins are seen frequently enough these days, but Hven take the highly unusual step (it may even be unique) of aging their spirit in oak *before* it is redistilled into gin. First, they make their own organic wheat-based spirit and then vat it for twenty-four hours with their botanicals.

After that, the spirit is filtered off and filled into American oak casks, where it matures for eighteen months. Then, into the tall Hven stills it goes – lots of extended copper contact and reflux going on there, I would guess, as the stills have unusually tall necks. All that sounds unusual enough, but the distillery then rest the chosen final cut for another three months in steel vats. And then, at which point even the most obsessive of us would have cried 'enough', they distil it again before reducing it to a bottling strength of 40% abv, but without carbon or chill filtration.

So this isn't a 'barrel aged' gin, but it is extraordinarily smooth, full flavoured and rich. Personally, I'd love to try it at 46% or even as a Navy Strength but I hesitate to tell someone this fanatical how to manage their business. The botanicals, including locally sourced juniper, comprise grains of paradise, citrus, aniseed, Guinea pepper, Sichuan pepper, calamus root, cardamom, cassia and Mauritian Bourbon vanilla (I did get a strong vanilla hit from this but assumed it was due to the pre-aging in American wood).

The flavours really do pop out very distinctly and clearly, but despite this Hven manages to be beautifully balanced and integrated. What's more, despite that time-consuming production method and rather charming packaging it's not absurdly expensive. UK websites offer this at around £32 for the 50cl bottle (equivalent to approximately £45 for a standard bottle). That's not cheap, but you'll want to sip and savour this most distinctive gin, which offers excellent value for the quality and presentation.

61

JENSEN'S BERMONDSEY DRY

BRAND OWNER: Bermondsey Distillery

DISTILLERY: Jensen's Bermondsey Distillery, Bermondsey, London

WEBSITE: www.bermondseygin.com

VISITOR CENTRE: Yes – Saturdays only

AVAILABILITY: Specialists

OTHER VARIANTS: Old Tom

Here's yet another exile from the world of high finance – and yet another product that has graduated from contract distillation by Thames Distillers to its own distillery. But, despite this and despite the modest bottle and simple label, this is not 'yet another' gin: that would be to greatly underestimate it.

The distillery's founder, Christian Jensen, discovered gin while working in Tokyo in banking IT. A bar there had the last few bottles of a largely forgotten London gin which had not been distilled for years – though, as it was to turn out, the brand name was still registered to one of the drinks industry's larger concerns and not available. But Jensen loved it, and on his return to his flat in Bermondsey, carrying with him what was believed to be the very last bottle, set about finding more. That search led him to an archive where, almost unbelievably, he was able to find the original recipe.

Thinking it would be fun to have a supply of his own personal gin and with no thoughts of commercialising the project, he took it to Charles Maxwell who soon replicated it. It's not a particularly complex recipe; in fact, it's an extremely old-fashioned London Dry using only old school botanicals: classical might be the best description. But, quietly and slowly at first, word spread: one after another better bars insisted they wanted to stock and serve it, and so more had to be produced.

Fast forward to 2015. Today, Jensen's Bermondsey gin is produced in Bermondsey in a specially designed John Dore stainless-steel-bodied still of 500-litres capacity with a copper cone head and lyne arm. It is operated by Bermondsey's distiller Dr Anne Brock, who, with her DPhil in Organic Chemistry from Oxford University, must be one of the most highly qualified people working in the industry today – but such is the level of skill and commitment that characterises this operation.

Another attraction at Bermondsey, which is conveniently close to Maltby Street and Borough Markets, is the opportunity to view Jensen's personal collection of gin ephemera. Far from jumping on today's craft distilling bandwagon, Jensen was one of the pioneers who made today's gin market a reality; whether that was the accidental consequence of a private enthusiasm or a cunning plan hardly matters.

We should all raise a glass to him and his splendid products.

JINZU

BRAND OWNER: Diageo plc

DISTILLERY: Cameronbridge, Fife

WEBSITE: www.diageobaracademy.com

VISITOR CENTRE: No

AVAILABILITY: Specialists

OTHER VARIANTS: None

For such a large company, Diageo can be remarkably imaginative and flexible. Take Jinzu, for example. It's a gin blended with premium sake. And it's not even their idea.

In their anxiety to curry favour with the bartending community, most drinks companies go to extraordinary lengths (top cocktail mixologists are treated even more reverently these days than drinks writers – not that I'm bitter). Think 'educational' distillery visits, regular cocktail competitions with lavish overseas trips and all kinds of goodies raining down on their heads, and you get the picture.

One such event is Diageo's Show Your Spirit competition. Bartenders are invited to present their idea for a new drink, which, if the winner impresses the judges, may be taken up and launched by Diageo – who pay the creator a royalty. And weird and wonderful ideas duly flow forth. In 2013, Dee Davies, a twenty-four-year-old Bristol barperson won the competition with 'Jin'.

After many months of development with Diageo's technical people, the distillers at Cameronbridge, and marketing and packaging agencies the result was launched as Jinzu. Described as 'a classically British gin with a Japanese twist', Jinzu is distilled in a traditional copper pot still where it combines typical gin botanicals with exotic botanicals from Japan. Naturally it leads with Tuscan juniper and coriander – essential to confirm its gin credentials. Then Japanese botanicals (yuzu citrus and cherry blossom) are added and distilled up to approximately 82%, after which Junmai sake is added and the spirit reduced to 41.3% for bottling. Why 41.3% I have no idea.

Apparently, Junmai is considered the 'single malt of sake'; the rice having been polished to 70% of its original size and its outer layers removed to ensure only the key flavours of the grain are maintained. At least, that's what I'm told. Sounds pretty convincing.

I wasn't entirely convinced when I read about this, but the pretty bottle got me half way to believing and the taste carried me over the line. East truly does meet West in this exciting fusion gin, so let's let Dee have the last word with her recommended serve: 'I prefer Jinzu as a dry Martini with a touch of plum wine to complement the botanicals but it makes a great Jin & Tonic with Fever Tree and a slice of green apple.'

Sounds nice, and I can confirm, it tastes nice.

63

JUNIPERO

BRAND OWNER: Anchor Distilling Company,
San Francisco

DISTILLERY: Old Potrero Distillery,
San Francisco, California, USA

WEBSITE: www.anchordistilling.com

VISITOR CENTRE: Yes

AVAILABILITY: Specialists

OTHER VARIANTS: Old Tom, Genevieve

Anchor Distilling represents a very interesting phenomenon – a business in transition from a somewhat quirky craft brewing and distilling operation, very much the creation of one driven individual to a larger, more corporate organisation. Junipero, one of the pioneers of small-batch gins, helped it get there.

It emerged from Anchor Brewing, a San Francisco craft brewer when the term was almost unknown, that had been saved from closure by Fritz Maytag, scion of a well-known domestic appliance company. Presumably brewing looked more fun than washing machines. Having got the brewery back on its feet, for some time prior to 1993 he had been toying with the idea of making rye whiskey, which had been almost forgotten as a style. Making it in a pot still, then a revolutionary concept for the US, worked well and led the team to further experimentation and exploration of distilling's history. From that apparently endless process it was but a small step to gin, from which thinking emerged Junipero, arguably the USA's first craft gin, launched in April of 1996.

You probably don't need me to tell you that it's a very juniper-led gin (the name's a bit of a giveaway). At the time, launching a pot still-distilled craft gin was radical enough without wild experimentation in unusual botanicals. The gin revolution as we now know it was yet to start – this lit the fuse but stayed within well-recognised boundaries. The idea was not to break the rules but to create a well-crafted product on an unusual production basis. In that goal Anchor succeeded, perhaps more fully than they anticipated.

At 49.3% Junipero is a forceful character, one well suited, like so many American craft gins, to mixing in a cocktail. There are twelve botanicals all worked together in the original small copper pot still. The exact mix is not disclosed, but one can detect a pronounced citrus impact, as well as the influence of coriander and what I take to be liquorice. But mainly this is about the juniper.

Maytag retired from the business in 2010.

It may be that, launched today, Junipero would not attract that much attention, but its remarkable place in the development of modern gin cannot pass unremarked.

64

LAKES

BRAND OWNER: The Lakes Distillery Company Ltd

DISTILLERY: The Lakes Distillery, Cumbria

WEBSITE: www.lakesdistillery.com

VISITOR CENTRE: Yes

AVAILABILITY: Limited

OTHER VARIANTS: None

Another day, another gin; another Oslo bottle. That's the trade name for this squat bottle which makes a regular appearance on the craft distilling scene (some bigger producers, such as Bruichladdich, even use it for whisky though their gin gets its own custom bottle). I've lost count of the number of these that I've seen.

Now, don't get me wrong: it's a very handsome bottle, simple and elegant, easy to use and I realise that the costs of a custom bottle are prohibitive for small operators. But (not to pick on Lakes because they're far from alone) the problem surely is one of distinct identity and stand-out shelf appeal. If lots of people use the same bottle then the label has to work extra hard. You might even come to pity the poor designer, which is not a sentence I ever expected to write. Anyway, as it's what's in the bottle that really counts and having made that point, I'll move on.

Lakes is a new distillery, having opened as recently as November 2014. It's based in and around some charming nineteenth-century farm buildings and seems to fit very naturally and comfortably into its landscape. MD and founder Paul Currie has family connections with the Arran distillery in Scotland (they make whisky there, of course) and has recruited some serious whisky distilling talent to run the operation here. It appears that they know a thing or two about making gin as well. Lakes is a slightly sweet drop that uses local botanicals such as bilberry, heather and meadowsweet to create a gin that is both smooth and engagingly complex. Juniper is ever present, naturally, but in this case it's locally sourced from the surrounding fells, and water comes from the River Derwent, so this is as artisanal and local as you get.

With the considerable Lake District tourist trade to boost their visitor numbers, all of them no doubt anxious to take home a souvenir rather more appealing than a copy of De Quincey's *Recollections*, the distillery's fame should spread far and wide.

Lakes show convincingly how far the new wave of distillers have advanced. This is a sophisticated, balanced and utterly convincing product that can hold its head up in any company. I'd suggest serving it just 50:50 with your tonic of choice. At 43.7% it's got plenty of mouthfeel, weight and body, and it's a shame to drown that with too much effervescence.

65

LANGLEY'S NO. 8

BRAND OWNER: Charter Brands Ltd

DISTILLERY: The Langley Distillery, Langley
Green, Warley, West Midlands

WEBSITE: www.langleysgin.com

VISITOR CENTRE: No

AVAILABILITY: Limited

OTHER VARIANTS: None

Langley's Distillery was founded almost a century ago by the Palmer family, who still own it today. Here since 1920 they have been developing and producing some of the finest award-winning gins in the world. In fact, another seven of the gins listed here start life in the West Midlands, coincidentally the same number that I've included from Thames Distillers. It's a substantial operation, with six stills and, though arguably less famous than Thames, is equally well regarded by those in the know.

But, as this carries the distillery's own name, you'd be forgiven for thinking it was their own brand. Not so: it's another contract distilled gin, this time for the Charter Brands company who wanted a gin for gentlemen, their theory being that many recently launched gins were too girly. That's not *quite* how they put it, but you get the idea – and you can make up your own mind.

The 'No. 8' tag came about because eight botanicals are used, and the eighth was the winning sample in their development trials, prior to the 2013 launch. It's made in 'Connie', a 4,000-litre English copper pot still from 1960 by John Dore & Company that wouldn't seem out of place in a single malt distillery. Unusually, the botanicals aren't steeped in the neutral grain spirit prior to distillation but placed directly in the still immediately prior to firing (men, eh, they just can't wait; gotta rush into everything).

The high-strength gin then leaves Warley for Witham in Essex where it is bottled at 41.7%. In researching all this I happened to note the curious coincidence that both Warley and Witham are mentioned in the Domesday Book. I don't suppose that's of the slightest significance, but it just struck me as curious and interesting. There's no charge, don't mention it.

What we can't avoid mentioning though is the 'gin for men' theory. Mark Dawkins, one of the men behind Charter Brands, has been so bold as to suggest that men have 'less of a sweet palate' and instead look for 'big flavours, complexity and a sophisticated flavour profile'. So, my wife being a total poppet, I thought I'd ask her.

'Interesting,' she said, 'but I don't want any more.' So there we have it: conclusive proof that my wife is definitely a woman.

66

MAKAR

BRAND OWNER: The Glasgow Distillery
Company Ltd
DISTILLERY: Glasgow Distillery, Glasgow
WEBSITE: www.glasgowdistillery.com
VISITOR CENTRE: No
AVAILABILITY: Limited
OTHER VARIANTS: None

Although this is a brand new distillery, it's backed by some serious and well-connected drinks industry personalities and is evidently well funded. If you doubt that, just take a look at the stylish customised bottle. Designs and a new bespoke glass mould don't come cheap, so this is a big statement of intent from the newly arrived Glasgow gin, named Makar, the Scots term for a poet or bard.

The venture, not to be confused with another rival Glasgow distillery which is about to start production on the banks of the River Clyde, is located in Hillington Business Park to the west of the city. Funding has come from a group of Asian food and drink investors as well as a £130,000 Regional Selective Assistance grant. Apparently, a total investment of 'several million' pounds was involved.

Though whisky stills will be installed, the Makar gin is produced in its brand new 450-litre Christian Carl still, a pot still with a seven-plate column that has been christened Annie. The still alone is a £100,000 piece of equipment, capable of producing some 300 bottles from each seven-hour distillation run. There is a first-year target of some 10,000 bottles, which is ambitious – but why not?

Many fine gins are made in Scotland, and this looks set fair to join that number. A traditionally styled dry gin, it's loaded with juniper berries and uses seven other botanicals: angelica root, rosemary, liquorice, peppercorns, coriander seeds, cassia bark and lemon peel. The distinctive bottle will certainly stand out on back bars, an increasingly important point of difference as the market for small-batch gins becomes ever more congested. The seven sides of the bottle are intended to represent the seven botanicals added to the juniper – and also make the bottle easy to grip and pour, which will no doubt be welcomed by harried bar staff.

Head distiller Jack Mayo, a graduate of the Heriot-Watt University's distilling course, is in charge of production and will be joined by David Robertson, ex-Macallan and Whyte & Mackay, on a consultancy basis once whisky production begins.

The taste is clearly, and very properly, described as 'juniper-led'; very markedly a world away from the lighter, more floral style of some new gins. Makar is bold, assertive and forceful – no mean gin, in fact.

67

MARTIN MILLER'S

BRAND OWNER:	The Reformed Spirits Company
DISTILLERY:	The Langley Distillery, Langley Green, Warley, West Midlands
WEBSITE:	www.martinmillersgin.com
VISITOR CENTRE:	No
AVAILABILITY:	Universal
OTHER VARIANTS:	Westbourne Strength (45.2%)

This highly awarded gin was one of the pioneers of the new wave of premium gins, and has been notably successful since its launch in 1999. It's probably an inspiration to today's craft distillers hoping to emulate its apparently effortless rise to fame.

The eponymous Martin Miller was a true English eccentric – *bon viveur*, photographer, author, publisher of Miller's Antique Guides, hotel proprietor and probably half a dozen other things as well – who apparently came up with the idea for his gin in 1998, after finding the gins then on the market fell short of his discriminating standards. So he decided to create his own. As you do. Well, you do now, but back then things were different: this was quite a radical proposition.

Two things make this stand out: first, the distillation. It's not that Martin Miller's employ a huge number of botanicals, or some arcane ingredient that no one has ever heard of; no, they simply split the process into two separate distillations. The juniper and the 'earthier' botanicals along with the dried lime peel are distilled first, then the citrus peels, and both distillates are combined later. This balances the signature notes of juniper, and the bright, refreshing notes of citrus. Again, not so unusual today, but somewhat unorthodox fifteen years ago. It does mean, however, that Martin Miller's doesn't qualify as a London Dry.

The next step remains, I think, unique. The high-strength distillate is reduced to drinking strength with water from Iceland. It seems like a lot of trouble to go to (in fact, you might almost consider it a gimmick), but the company argues that the normal de-mineralised water is 'dead', despite accounting for around 50% to 60% of the contents.

According to the company, Icelandic Spring Water (they have their own spring now) is 'simply the purest and softest naturally occurring water to be found on the planet', which qualities make it perfect for blending gin. All this shipping water across the high seas might strike you as expensive, and so you'd expect Martin Miller's to be pricey. Actually, you can find it widely available for £25 or less; not the cheapest then, but hardly overpriced.

Lots more information on their generally excellent website, though I do think it's slightly morbid of them not to have dropped the 'Ask Martin' page now that the fellow has gone to the great cocktail bar in the sky – where I imagine he's thoroughly enjoying himself.

MGC

BRAND OWNER:	The Melbourne Gin Company
DISTILLERY:	Melbourne Gin Company, Gembrook, Victoria, Australia
WEBSITE:	www.melbournegincompany.com
VISITOR CENTRE:	No
AVAILABILITY:	Only stocked in a handful of bars and shops
OTHER VARIANTS:	None

There is a burgeoning craft distilling industry in Australia that has enjoyed great success, especially the single malt whiskies from Tasmania: most cannot keep up with demand, so great has been the consumer response.

Here's a gin, distilled near Melbourne, that since its launch in July 2013 has proved an overnight success in better bars in its home country, and which I fully expect to see making waves here on the UK bar scene – if only they can make enough.

Distiller Andrew Marks, who comes from a background of winemaking (which he still pursues), references Frank Moorhouse's book *Martini – A Memoir*, with its description of the perfect Martini: 'Every time it is served, the Martini represents a journey towards an unattainably ideal drink.' Andrew's fascination with Martinis and all things gin led him to delve into the mysteries of gin production, beginning his experiments on a small scale back in 2009.

The notion of the 'unattainable ideal drink' spurred a series of trials and experiments and the extraction of exotic and local botanicals. The MGC doffs its hat to London Dry Gin with the two major components being juniper berries and coriander seed. There are eleven botanicals in total, with the grapefruit peel and rosemary coming from the garden at Andrew's Gembrook Hill Vineyard. The other botanicals are macadamia, sandalwood, honey lemon myrtle and organic navel orange, which are all sourced from Australia, alongside angelica root, orris root and cassia bark.

Each botanical is distilled separately and then blended to the MGC recipe – essentially a winemakers' approach. Seeking to preserve the delicate nature of the botanicals, Andrew works with a copper pot bain-marie alembic from Portugal (the type of still traditionally used for making perfume).

The final, determinedly local component is the pure and fresh Gembrook rainwater, which, they maintain, allows the botanicals to shine through. At only 60kms from Melbourne this local source contributes to the unique 'Melbourne Dry Gin' style.

MGC is very approachable, sippable in its own right, delightfully balanced between the sweet notes, citrus and classic gin botanicals. Great in a G&T, of course, but it really performs in the orange-dominated Martinez.

69

MONKEY 47

BRAND OWNER: Black Forest Distillers

DISTILLERY: Black Forest, Lossburg, Germany

WEBSITE: www.Monkey47.com

VISITOR CENTRE: No

AVAILABILITY: Limited

OTHER VARIANTS: Distiller's Cut (annual limited edition)

Here's something clearly put together by someone quite obsessive. I mean that in a good way, because I really did love every 'touch point' (a bit of marketing jargon there for you) about the brand even before I opened the bottle.

And then I positively squealed with pleasure because there is a little silver-coloured metal collar mounted on the cork, and, if you squint at it, you will find a Latin motto engraved there. *Ex pluribus unum*, it reads, which I take to mean 'out of many, one' – a reference no doubt to the forty-seven different botanicals (including *six* different peppers – I mean, come on) that go into this uniquely German gin which, as you will have guessed, is bottled at 47% abv. And, if you look even more closely, the metal collar is exquisitely engraved and there are delicate little crosses separating the text. You really have to be slightly mad to go to this trouble – and I love it.

You might think the bottle owes something to Hendrick's and the label to Elephant (or perhaps *vice versa*), but the product is unique. Of course, every product is unique, but this is really different. Their website is a thing of joy, on which you can happily spend hours reading about many different species of monkey, the jazz of Oscar Peterson, cork trees, Eddie the Eagle, many, many different cocktail recipes and their history, various different botanicals and the origins of Monkey 47. Incredibly, it can be traced to the personal recipe of a British RAF officer, Wing Commander Montgomery Collins who settled in the Black Forest in the 1950s with the aim of becoming a watchmaker.

Fortunately for us, he apparently wasn't very good at it, so opened a guesthouse instead, which he named The Wild Monkey in honour of Max, a monkey he had sponsored in Berlin Zoo immediately after the war. There he attempted to recreate English gin, but with added local ingredients.

Thinking about all that, he must have been a true British eccentric. His spirit (pun intended) has been captured by founder Alexander Stein and his splendidly hirsute master distiller Christoph Keller, who, in recreating Collins' recipe, makes what wine critic Robert Parker called 'the greatest gin I have ever tasted'. Astonishingly, after distillation, the spirit rests for three months in earthenware crocks before it's reduced for bottling. I told you they were obsessive.

A highly distinctive product then, but a wonderful one.

NB

BRAND OWNER: North Berwick Distillery Ltd
DISTILLERY: North Berwick, East Lothian
WEBSITE: www.nbgin.com
VISITOR CENTRE: No
AVAILABILITY: Limited
OTHER VARIANTS: Navy Strength (limited edition)

N.B. *Nota bene.* It's the Latin for 'note well', a phrase which first appeared in text around 1721. 'Pay attention' it says.

And if we were in Scotland we might remember that Scotland once more or less happily referred to itself as NB, 'North Britain', hence the nomenclature of Edinburgh's grandest of grand railway hotels, the North British. Today it has sadly rebranded itself into the anodyne Balmoral Hotel. Which, as any Scot could tell you, ought by rights to be on Deeside.

NB also stands for North Berwick, a pleasant seaside town right on the Forth Estuary, about twenty-five miles east of Edinburgh and once a fashionable seaside resort. I have fond memories of North Berwick because in another life I played a role in establishing the town's principal attraction, the Scottish Seabird Centre.

And now it has something else – its very own distillery; a little one, with a John Dore still (not many of those about), making around one hundred litres per batch of NB Gin. It's a pretty straight-along-the-line London Dry gin, using just eight botanicals: juniper, coriander seed, angelica root, grains of paradise, lemon peel, cassia bark, cardamom and orris root. As you might expect, it's pretty much old school in style (nothing wrong with that), with plenty of juniper and orange notes, and bottled at a sensible 42% abv.

The distillery is the brainchild of husband and wife team Steve and Viv Muir, who have taken a very hands-on role at their micro-distillery, since launching it in October 2013. It's found a ready local acceptance and even made it into some export markets, despite the rather basic packaging. Oh, all right, it's minimalist, or retro or something. It does come in a box, if you're concerned about that kind of thing.

I'd rate this a very decent cocktail gin. Apparently Charles Maxwell of Thames Distillers advised on the development tasting panel, which was pretty decent of him, and rated it 'a very fine gin that was extremely likeable'. It's gone on to win a Silver Medal at the 2014 Gin Masters competition.

So, you see, NB does stand for 'pay attention' after all. Given a decent sea breeze behind it I expect to see more of NB Gin.

NOLET'S SILVER DRY

BRAND OWNER: C H J Nolet BV, Schiedam,
The Netherlands

DISTILLERY: Nolet's Distillery, Schiedam,
The Netherlands

WEBSITE: www.noletsgin.com

VISITOR CENTRE: Yes

AVAILABILITY: Specialists

OTHER VARIANTS: Reserve Dry

Founded in 1691, the Nolet Distillery is a family-owned company with roots going back ten generations from father to son. The current chairman is Carel Nolet; his sons Carel Jr and Bob, representing the eleventh generation, both work in the company. Their most famous product today is Ketel One Vodka, a huge seller in the USA, now a 50/50 joint venture operation with Diageo.

But using their own wheat-based neutral spirit and a small Holstein still, they also make this rather interesting and slightly controversial gin. It does rather stretch the gin definition – not as far as, say, Hoxton, but it is not your run-of-the-mill juniper-led gin either. They have consciously moved to some unusual botanicals, notably white peach, raspberry and Turkish rose, which are added as essences, prepared for them in France. The result definitely polarises opinion.

While the quality and distilling heritage can hardly be questioned, to be generous, this is a very contemporary spirit, challenging expectations of what to expect from a gin. In that regard, and especially considering the use of rose in the recipe, it does remind one of Hendrick's. That undoubtedly brought new drinkers who 'don't like gin' into the gin camp and this, no doubt, is what lies behind Nolet's thinking. They also devote considerable effort to promoting the brand in the USA, perhaps in the view that the market there will be more receptive to the experimental.

It's also a market where the cocktail culture is arguably more broadly spread, and here lies part of the explanation for the taste – it's designed to work well in a range of mixed drinks and to appeal to the bartending community who are, of course, already well disposed to Nolet because of the success of Ketel One. The role of the bartender, especially in US bar culture, is not to be underestimated, something that the Nolet marketing team know very well.

Though bottled at 47.6%, you will find this is very much at the top of the price band for gin – expect to pay over £60 for a bottle. That, however, starts to look quite the bargain when compared to Nolet's ultra-premium, ultra-rare Reserve Dry. Sold almost exclusively in the USA, if you have to ask the price you can't afford it.

OK, it's around $700 (currently about £460). Still want one?

72

NO. 1 LONDON ORIGINAL

BRAND OWNER:	Gonzalez Byass SA
DISTILLERY:	Thames Distillers, Timbermill Distillery, Clapham, London
WEBSITE:	www.thelondon1.com
VISITOR CENTRE:	No
AVAILABILITY:	Specialists
OTHER VARIANTS:	None

The first thing you notice, of course, is the turquoise colour of this gin. It's actually less marked in the product itself than in photography but it's still rather peculiar, and, to me at least, off-putting (especially if you remember that gin used to have the nickname 'blue ruin' – a not particularly flattering reference to poor-quality spirit). But I suppose it's by way of drawing attention to the bottle which is an off-the-shelf number used by quite a number of spirits brands and, of itself, somewhat lacking in originality of thought (though the slim, wrap-round label is nice enough).

So why is it blue? Because they macerate gardenia flowers in it is the technical answer, but I think I've already covered the real reason in my first paragraph. Though this is distilled in London, calls itself 'The London Gin' and for good measure backs that up with 'No. 1 Original' and a neck logo from 'The London Gin Company Ltd' (it's not shy about coming forward as you've noticed) it's not actually a London Gin in terms of the definition. I thought I'd better point that out in case you might foolishly imagine they were trying to suggest otherwise.

Distilled by Charles Maxwell of Thames Distillers (who we have met more than once in these pages) at a robust 47%, it's part of an effort by the Spanish sherry producers Gonzalez Byass to broaden their portfolio and capitalise on the worldwide boom for crafted spirits. They are not alone in this ambition.

Some years ago their rivals Williams & Humbert launched A F Cricketer's Gin, in a rather more stylish bottle with a label design by the great Michael Peters. Perhaps this effort will be more successful than A F Cricketer's, which came too early to benefit from the gin revival, did not trouble the scorer, and is now in the great gin pavilion in the sky. Were it around today I suspect it could do rather well: older connoisseurs of mothers' ruin still speak highly of it.

That's by the by. I simply wanted to make the point that this isn't an entirely original business idea and I should have been sorry if this book made it into print without some mention of A F Cricketer's. As for No. 1, well, it wouldn't be my first choice though it might make it into the Second XI (time to 'retire' the lame cricketing references, *Ed.*).

73

NO. 3 LONDON DRY

BRAND OWNER: Berry Brothers & Rudd

DISTILLERY: De Kuyper Royal, Schiedam, The Netherlands

WEBSITE: www.no3gin.com

VISITOR CENTRE: No, but a lovely shop at 3 St James's Street, Mayfair, London

AVAILABILITY: Specialists

OTHER VARIANTS: None

What more traditional, upper-crust symbol of London could you find than Berry Brothers & Rudd's delightfully antiquated shop at 3 St James's Street in the very heart of Mayfair? Over 300 years of tradition seep from its hallowed walls. They have long quenched the British ruling class's thirst with claret and other fine beverages, and they were responsible for creating Cutty Sark, one of the great cocktail whiskies.

And is there a better example of the traditional, juniper-led gin style than their No. 3 London Dry Gin? There are the words, right on the front of the elegant, dark green bottle. It could hardly be plainer.

But wait a moment. There's a slight problem: the bottle gives the hint, for it's in the shape of an old-fashioned genever. Which, of course, hails from the Low Countries. Which are not in London. And it turns out that this very fine, inimitably English gin is, in fact, distilled for Berry's in Holland which, of course, is where gin's story started.

However, in his ever-so-excellent *Difford's Gin Compendium*, writer and cocktail geek extraordinaire Simon Difford calls for the protection of an appellation for the term 'London Dry Gin'. He laments the fact that London Dry – being a style, not geographically defined, like Xoriguer – 'can be adopted by gins made all over the world'.

In a perfect world, I think he's right. Unfortunately, it's not going to happen, and London Dry now belongs to the world. If only they were all as good as this. Berry's Dutch partners have created what they are pleased to call 'the absolute embodiment of what a London Dry Gin should be', and some noted gin connoisseurs agree.

So should we be worried? In truth, probably not. London is probably big enough to soak up any damage to its reputation and, conversely, to take the kudos arising from superb products such as this. It is light years away from more 'modern' gins such as Bombay Sapphire, and the very antithesis of gins such as Hendrick's, but remains very much in style for all of that.

This, then, is a classic, made with the minimum of botanicals, no gimmicky ingredients and presented with understated authority. You sense that Berry Brothers & Rudd, having been around for 300 years, plan to stick around for another 300. And, with products like this, they might do just that.

74

OLD ENGLISH

BRAND OWNER:	Hammer & Son, Fredericksberg, Denmark
DISTILLERY:	The Langley Distillery, Langley Green, Warley, West Midlands
WEBSITE:	www.oldenglishgin.com
VISITOR CENTRE:	No
AVAILABILITY:	Limited
OTHER VARIANTS:	None

Here's an odd thing: gin in a champagne bottle, made to a recipe dating from 1783 that is apparently kept in a safe. I do wonder why marketing people imagine these things are important or why they bother to tell us stuff like that. They must imagine we're captivated by these romantic stories and believe that they cast a soft, comforting glow of provenance and heritage onto their products. Oh wait, we are, and they do.

Old English is another creation from that Great Dane Henrik Hammer, in which he is attempting to suggest how English (as opposed to Hollands, i.e. Dutch) gin might have looked and tasted in the eighteenth century. He noted that England was the largest importer of champagne back then (we still get through a fair amount) and hypothesised that bottles, being expensive objects at the time, would have been taken to gin shops to be refilled with a drop of kill-grief. It's a perfectly reasonable guess, I suppose, though what archaeologists and social historians would make of it I have no idea.

How accurately it replicates the gin of 1783 I wouldn't care to speculate. The recipe is doubtless authentic, but so many other things will have changed: the quality of the base spirit and botanicals and the detailed control of the process to mention but two. But then again, it doesn't really matter – what counts is whether or not today this counts as a decent gin.

It's a distilled gin, that's to say sugar is added after the distillation, which has used a fairly conventional mix of botanicals: juniper, coriander, lemon, orange, angelica, cassia, liquorice, cinnamon, orris root, nutmeg and cardamom, all distilled in a 100% English wheat pure grain spirit in Langley's Angela still.

Between Hammer and the team at Langley's they do know their stuff, and Old English has collected a number of impressive awards in high-class competition. Strictly speaking, this is an Old Tom but perhaps not as sweet as some. So, a decent replica of a 200-year-old-plus recipe, but personally I would have passed on the driven cork – faithfulness to the original can go too far and you're unlikely to drink the bottle at a sitting.

In today's age of responsible drinking that would be taking eighteenth-century authenticity a step too far. I couldn't possibly condone that, boys and girls, so please don't try it at home.

75

OPIHR

BRAND OWNER: Quintessential Brands

DISTILLERY: G & J Distillers, Warrington

WEBSITE: www.opihr.com

VISITOR CENTRE: No

AVAILABILITY: Limited

OTHER VARIANTS: None

Right, before we get started on this, the fourth entry from Quintessential, and another new gin from master distiller Joanne Moore (clearly a lady with a restless and inventive mind), let's begin by saluting the marketing brain behind this.

For surely this is a marketing creation, even if the gin itself is a product of the distillery. The get-up is very pleasing; both bottle and label design are deceptively simple (that takes a lot of skill, believe me) and the whole package has a tactile quality that's hard to resist. They call it 'shelf-appeal' in the trade. Someone has then come up with a load of half-believable guff on the website and back label describing Opihr as 'a legendary region famed for its wealth and riches which prospered during the reign of King Solomon. The king regularly received cargoes of gold, silver and spices from Opihr and while its exact location remains a mystery, it is thought to have been in the Orient along the ancient Spice Route.' Well, I suppose since the whole thing is a legend it could as well have been in Timbuktu or darkest Neasden for that matter (possibly not Neasden). It's generally spelled Ophir; I haven't the slightest idea why they saw fit to change it.

Opihr – it's pronounced 'o-peer' by the way, though under the influence of H Rider Haggard I still badly want to spell it Ophir – is apparently targeted at 24–35-year-olds with a sense of adventure. That would seem to rule me out. It's certainly not going to appeal to the Jaguar-driving golf-club set that could be considered the archetypal gin drinker (though I don't fit in there either). Whatever, as I've been told adventurous 24–35-year-olds might say.

Right there on the label, centre front, are the words 'Oriental Spiced'. So the mighty hit of cardamom and pepper that envelop your nose as you open the bottle shouldn't come as a surprise, even if the idea of a spiced gin is mildly shocking. With their recent releases, Quintessential really are pushing at our understanding of what gin should be.

I think I part company with the producer here. Not that this isn't interesting and different – and I'd urge you to try it, because it may just be your personal treasure galleon – but because for me the spice notes of cardamom, cumin and coriander are overwhelming and unsubtle. In fact, to be honest, I'm not sure I can really distinguish them individually.

Perhaps I should be more adventurous. I still think it's a very nice pack, though.

OXLEY

BRAND OWNER:	Oxley Spirits Company (Bacardi)
DISTILLERY:	Oxley Spirits Company (Thames Distillers Ltd for Bacardi) Thames Distillers, Timbermill Distillery, Clapham, London
WEBSITE:	www.oxleygin.com
VISITOR CENTRE:	Certainly not!
AVAILABILITY:	Very limited
OTHER VARIANTS:	None

This rather beautifully packaged super-premium gin is actually a Bacardi product – not that you would know that from its low-profile approach. I wanted to see it being made, so I asked to visit the distillery. I enquired, politely I thought. Their marketing man recoiled in horror. 'That won't be possible.'

I like a challenge, so, just a few days later, I breezed nonchalantly onto a nondescript south London industrial estate sandwiched between a timber merchant and some rail tracks, trying hard not to be noticed (marketing men have spies everywhere). Once past an intimidating security barrier, had marketing man been watching, he would have seen two middle-aged chaps enter a large metal shed, with all the glamour of a run-down Northern carpet warehouse.

But appearances are not everything; for here I saw the Oxley Cold Distillation process. The still – unrecognisable as such – appears to be something from the laboratory of *Back to the Future* inventor Dr Emmett Brown. But from it flows slowly – excruciatingly slowly – a gin of sublime delicacy and refinement, so perfectly smooth, fresh, creamy and utterly mouth-watering that as I write this I am consuming a good tumblerful, neat and at room temperature. Bad Ian.

Vacuum distillation is not entirely unknown, but Oxley have combined this with a gizmo that forces the spirit vapour to hit a cold thingy (I promised not to reveal the technical secrets). And by 'cold' I mean *cold*. Colder than penguin's feet. Colder than an unimaginably cold thing on Planet Cold.

This means that the spirit retains all the delicacy and freshness of the botanicals, which include, most unusually, fresh grapefruit, orange and lemon. When you uncork the bottle you get a delicious burst of enticing citrus notes entreating you to 'drink me, drink me'. Apparently they had thirty-eight goes at the recipe. They got it right, if you ask me.

Don't worry if it looks expensive at around £50. It's a litre bottle of 47% deliciousness. Actually, they should charge more. That's not something I say very often, so hopefully the marketing man will forgive me now. Sorry about visiting the distillery.

77

PLYMOUTH

BRAND OWNER: Coates & Company
(Pernod Ricard)

DISTILLERY: Black Friars Distillery, Plymouth, Devon

WEBSITE: www.plymouthgin.com

VISITOR CENTRE: Yes

AVAILABILITY: Widespread

OTHER VARIANTS: Also available as Navy Strength (57% abv) and Sloe Gin style

Hello, sailor! Back in 1896, Plymouth Gin was specified in the earliest documented recipe for a Dry Martini (I expect you're shaken but not stirred). Despite the early fame, this grand old brand ended up as a makeweight in a series of corporate deals, passing from hand to hand through a series of uncomprehending and largely uncaring owners. It was probably too small and insignificant for anyone to even notice, and so escaped rationalisation and closure until eventually it came into the hands of Pernod Ricard. They own Beefeater and know and care about gin.

The interesting fact about Plymouth is that while London Gin can be produced anywhere (because it's a style), since a court action in the 1880s Plymouth has only been produced in the city itself. The legal action, against a number of London-based distillers who were selling 'Plymouth' gin, suggests the name itself had some cachet. (Note: if starting a new boutique distillery it might be an idea to do it there). For some years the brand enjoyed Protected Geographical Origin status in EU law, but the relevant geographical indicator has now lapsed, though production remains firmly at the Black Friars distillery.

Due perhaps to the soft Dartmoor water, the Plymouth style is somewhat sweeter than the classic London Dry style, possessing deep earthy notes and a wonderfully fresh juniper and lemony bite. It has a slight sweetness due to the selection of botanicals with extraordinary concentration and complexity. No single botanical dominates the overall flavour.

Beloved of the Royal Navy, especially when served with Angostura bitters as the enduring Pink Gin, Plymouth Gin is now enjoying something of a revival (which is just as well as our Navy now seems to consist of not very much at all) in smarter cocktail bars and amongst gin drinkers looking for something a little offbeat but not so *outré* as might scandalise the vicar.

After its various vicissitudes, this famous old brand looks well settled in its new home and happy in its new packaging (I never really understood or liked the brief flirtation with the *faux*-Art Deco bottle which was neither stylish nor reflected Plymouth's heritage).

If your taste runs to a stronger tot, try Plymouth's Navy Strength (57%) – a right old howitzer amongst gins, very highly rated by aficionados and top cocktail barmen (OK, mixologists).

PORTOBELLO ROAD

BRAND OWNER: Leelex Ltd, Leeds, Yorkshire
DISTILLERY: Thames Distillers, Timbermill Distillery, Clapham, London
WEBSITE: www.portobellostarbar.co.uk
VISITOR CENTRE: Yes (Ginstitute Museum)
AVAILABILITY: Widespread
OTHER VARIANTS: None

With several hundred gin brands now on the market, and more arriving every week, it's genuinely hard to create something new that has the vital point of difference that will pull in drinkers – and that's if you can convince the notoriously hard-bitten trade buyers who are constantly being pitched new ideas. Which, of course, they take great relish in crushing with their renowned cynicism, world-class brutality and calculated cruelty (like publishers, really, but even less charming).

So, for Portobello Road to have come up with a brand as recently as autumn 2011 that is already being stocked in at least one major supermarket is a considerable achievement; all the more so when in essence it came about accidentally. When proprietors Ged Feltham and Jake Burger were experimenting with (very) small-scale distilling for their Ginstitute Museum located above their Portobello Star pub this product took on a life of its own. And that is all the more remarkable when you consider that at that stage they were essentially pub and club operators and the museum was simply an idea to fill empty floors above the Portobello Star.

Today, the Ginstitute is the place to go in London to learn more about gin. Ged and Jake created it to hold their collection of vintage gins and to provide the opportunity for visitors to blend their own bespoke gin. To do that they needed a variety of distillates, which they prepared in their tiny Portuguese pot still (similar in style to the ones at 58 and Tarquin's) – but before long they had also created a classy London Dry with gin's long-time favourite botanicals joined, unusually, by nutmeg.

Cutting a long story short, that very soon found favour with buyers here and abroad, and production had to be turned over to Charles Maxwell at Thames Distillers who was able to scale up the quantities in his Tom Thumb still. However, it's not just the gin – excellent though it is – that stands out.

The bottle resembles a classic cognac bottle and the label, clearly designed with a great love of Victorian graphics, combines nostalgia with contemporary shelf appeal and visual impact. In a crowded market, nothing else looks quite like Portobello Road, and that is a very hard trick to pull off.

79

PROFESSOR CORNELIUS AMPLEFORTH'S BATHTUB GIN

BRAND OWNER:	Atom Supplies Ltd
DISTILLERY:	Prof. Cornelius Ampleforth's Compounding Works, Tunbridge Wells
WEBSITE:	www.masterofmalt.com
VISITOR CENTRE:	No
AVAILABILITY:	Specialists
OTHER VARIANTS:	Navy Strength, Old Tom, Sloe, Cask Aged, Cask Aged Navy

If nothing else, you've got to admit the name is unusual. But stick with me, it's also tasty.

The story goes that back in 2011 Professor Cornelius Ampleforth fulfilled a lifelong ambition when he released his extraordinary Bathtub Gin. Not content with this highly successful experiment, he proceeded to lock himself back inside his laboratory and set about on all manner of additional, exciting projects. The result was an entire range of original and reimagined spirits inspired by bygone eras and modern technology alike. Whether it's cold compounding or distillation under vacuum, the madcap professor does whatever it takes to produce the finest libations and retain the freshness of the wonderful botanicals he uses. Or so they say . . .

I'll let you into a secret: there isn't really a Professor Ampleforth (sorry if you're disappointed), but if it helps, think of him as a sort of Santa Claus of gin, showering us with all kinds of goodies. The range, which keeps growing, is the brainchild of a well-known, dynamic and irreverent web-based drinks retailer who consistently surprise with their unconventional offerings.

But they are not simply wacky and experimental for the sake of it. These products are thoughtfully constructed and logically conceived to explore and showcase different aspects of gin's personality. Cold compounding would generally be sniffed at as the lowest form of gin manufacture. Many of the products are cold vacuum distilled, which is more complex and technically demanding. So, underneath the carefully cultivated offbeat image is a well thought-out set of varying expressions from a young and enthusiastic team who truly care about what they are doing (while trying not to show it too obviously; quite an English attitude if you think about it).

So, kudos to them. And praise for the packaging, which is fun. And high praise for their policy of offering all these products in 3cl sample bottles, which allow you to try them at minimal risk of an expensive mistake. Find them at masterofmalt.com

And, if my word's not good enough, the World Gin Awards 2014 declared the Bathtub Gin to be the World's Best Compound Gin. Not bad for a mad professor from Tunbridge Wells (perhaps, like Santa, he does exist after all).

80

RANSOM OLD TOM

BRAND OWNER: Ransom Spirits

DISTILLERY: Ransom Spirits, Sheridan, Oregon, USA

WEBSITE: www.ransomspirits.com

VISITOR CENTRE: No

AVAILABILITY: Specialists

OTHER VARIANTS: Ransom Dry, Small's Gin

Here's an old Old Tom. But it tells you all you need to know that this was launched as recently as 2009 and was only the second such gin in this style available in the modern age (Hayman's was the first). Confusingly, it's very different from its predecessor, being aged where that is not and unsweetened where Hayman's add a dose of sugar. The base spirit differs as well. So who has found the secret to an authentic Old Tom?

Probably both. Hayman's had the benefit of actually having made the style up until the 1950s so could refer to an original recipe, whereas the Ransom version was developed after painstaking research in conjunction with drinks historian David Wondrich, working to retro-engineer an Old Tom based on vintage cocktail recipes. It was he who set Ransom's owner and distiller Tad Seestedt on the quest to recreate a little bit of history.

Seestedt had started Ransom in 1997 with, as he says, his 'small life savings and a fistful of credit cards'. The name was chosen to represent the debt incurred to start the business! Today, the company is located on a forty-acre farm where they tend their own organic vines and grow barley for their whiskeys.

Great emphasis is laid on historical authenticity, craftsmanship and *terroir* as the distillery's core values, and the Old Tom expression exemplifies that. The aim here was to create a product that would work in cocktails popular in the mid-nineteenth century, so this is very much a niche product, tailored to a very specific market.

Whether it would have appealed to the original drinkers of Old Tom some hundred years or so ago I leave to your imagination – but they don't sound too discriminating. The name reputedly originated with the infamous Captain Dudley Bradstreet, who I think I may now safely call a rogue and a scoundrel. In a cunning attempt to avoid the restrictions of the Gin Act, Dudley ingeniously sold drams of gin by mounting a device in the shape of a cat's paw on a London doorway. Passers-by inserted a suitable coin and called out 'Puss' then received the liquid via a pipe; presumably they drank it there and then. Soon, the image of a black cat was linked to Old Tom gin – or so the story goes.

It's all very different today. Ransom's version is a scholarly recreation of gin's history, enabling you to enjoy its charms while persuading yourself that you are engaged in serious 'research'.

81

ROCK ROSE

BRAND OWNER: Dunnet Bay Distillers Ltd,
Thurso, Caithness

DISTILLERY: Dunnet Bay, Thurso, Caithness

WEBSITE: www.rockrosegin.co.uk

VISITOR CENTRE: Yes

AVAILABILITY: Limited

OTHER VARIANTS: None

Here's a truly hand-crafted Scottish gin that, in just its first few weeks, achieved quite a splash of attention and made a healthy start on the goal to sell 10,000 bottles a year (that's a lot for a small, start-up operation). What's more, it's in about as remote a location as you can imagine anywhere in mainland Britain and, while setting it up, co-founder Martin Murray spent around half his time on an oil rig in the North Sea where he worked as a process engineer.

That's a big part of the success. Having qualified at Heriot-Watt University, Martin and wife Claire longed to return home to Caithness and set up their own brewing and distilling business. So Martin obtained further experience with the university's School of Brewing and Distilling and, after a lot of research and trials, was able to set up his own Dunnet Bay distillery in late 2014.

The still was manufactured to a unique design by John Dore & Company and features an unusual stainless-steel body with a copper dome and column; the result is efficient heating, combined with lots of copper contact in the condensing phase – so important to flavour in the spirit. All the botanicals are contained in a separate Carterhead-style basket to preserve the delicacy of the locally sourced ingredients.

They too are a little unusual: as well as the regulation juniper and the more conventional cardamom, Martin and Claire are using rose root, sea buckthorn, rowan (keeps away the witches, as we know) and blaeberries. The result of these, and a few secret others, together with long, slow distillation and vapour infusion, is a light, fragrant and floral gin with a most attractive and distinctive nose that doesn't lack for body or mouthfeel.

A small business such as this has an inbuilt advantage at the capital investment stage as it can qualify for substantial grants from Scotland's enterprise agencies (as this did). But it still requires great personal commitment of time and money (well over £100,000 in this case) and the challenges of the remote location never go away. I checked, and the distillery is more than 270 miles (over six hours' hard driving) from Edinburgh's Bramble Bar, a great gin joint.

If ever you make it to John O'Groats, take the time to visit the distillery: their Rock Rose gin is a very fine product indeed, one that speaks volumes about what can be achieved with talent, energy and some lovely local botanicals.

82

SACRED

BRAND OWNER:	Sacred Spirits Company Ltd
DISTILLERY:	Sacred, Highgate, London
WEBSITE:	www.sacredspiritscompany.com
VISITOR CENTRE:	No (private house)
AVAILABILITY:	Specialists
OTHER VARIANTS:	Christmas Pudding, Pink Grapefruit, Cardamom, Juniper, Negroni Giftpack, Gin Blending Kit

Imagine if you will, gin as a work of art, something that the Tate Gallery might exhibit. No need – it exists. But this is an exhibit that you get to consume – making you, you might say, part of the artwork itself. Yes, the Tate actually has its own gin, which you can enjoy in their bar and restaurant.

And, if the idea appeals, you can actually become the artist yourself, creating your own utterly unique bespoke gin from the gin blending kit that Sacred will sell you. One of the very first micro-distilling operations, Sacred aim to sell around 1,000 bottles a week in 2015 – not bad for a distillery that operates from a room in a private house in North London and was only established in 2009.

Joint owner and distiller Ian Hart is another refugee from the City, a former master of the universe who turned to distilling when the financial world broke bad. Perhaps he, Daniel Szor (Cotswold) and Robin Gerlach (Elephant) should form an escape committee to persuade more of their former colleagues to turn to the way of the still. Fewer bankers and more distillers, that would be my recipe for greater Gross National Happiness.

Actually, Sacred does in many ways exemplify the GNH approach to life. Everything is produced by hand on their table-top, low-pressure cold vacuum distilling apparatus – a rota-vap to the technically minded. Nothing is rushed: the twelve botanicals at the heart of Sacred's gins are all macerated for up to a month and a half before being distilled separately then blended to individual recipes and bottled at 40%.

Just five years ago the idea of cold distilling under a vacuum seemed eccentric and probably doomed to failure. But the quality of Sacred's products soon convinced bartenders that here was something special, and others took note. Now, brands such as Oxley and Professor Cornelius Ampleforth use a similar technique, and it is, in part at least, also seen at the Dodd's and Half Hitch distilleries.

Cold distillation maintains the freshness and vibrancy of the more delicate botanicals, a signature note in Sacred's products. With his meticulous small-batch approach and insistence on hands-on production, Ian Hart is not going to conquer the world of gin but he has the satisfaction of having changed it.

His are landmark products that every gin lover should try. Works of art, you might even say.

83

SAFFRON

BRAND OWNER: Gabriel Boudier

DISTILLERY: Boudier, Dijon, France

WEBSITE: www.boudier.com

VISITOR CENTRE: No

AVAILABILITY: Specialists

OTHER VARIANTS: Rare London Dry

You probably know Gabriel Boudier for their Crème de Cassis de Dijon – a product so highly esteemed they were awarded the Légion d'honneur, France's highest decoration. Think of it as the nearest thing to a republican Royal Warrant and you'll get the idea.

They have been making their liqueurs since 1874 so they know a thing or two about distilling. The company is still family owned and distinctively French in style – something expressed wonderfully well in their ornate labels. Saffron Gin's label is quite restrained by their standards but, delightfully, is actually printed on tin, not paper, an idiosyncratic touch that I greatly appreciated. But that, of course, is not what you first notice about this gin . . .

Yes, it's the colour – uncomfortably close to a glass of Irn-Bru, not that that distinctively Scottish beverage is frequently poured in Dijon, or indeed in the sophisticated cocktail bars that are the natural habitat of this product. The colour is derived from saffron, reputedly the most expensive of spices and one that was apparently used in the nineteenth century in a recipe discovered in the Boudier archive. Though we think of India during this period as a British colony, there were French outposts in Pondichéry, Chandernagor and Madras, and Indian spices were imported to Europe where they would have found their way into gin.

Whether because of cost or because it doesn't seem to me at least to sit well in gin, saffron never really established a place as a key botanical and isn't much used today. Diplôme and Cadenhead's Old Raj Gin, with their pale straw colour, are the only other ones that come to mind. Other than that, the botanicals in Boudier's version are fairly conventional: juniper, coriander, lemon, orange peel, angelica seeds, iris and fennel all feature. The saffron is added after distillation, making this a distilled gin probably best enjoyed in a cocktail (a Negroni, with its orange twist works rather well).

Saffron Gin, despite its distinguished producer, is something of an outlier. Its colour marks it out from other gins and will offend the purist. It doesn't feel that well balanced to me, and the saffron tends to dominate and mask the other flavours. It's certainly one to try, however, but probably more as an occasional novelty rather than forming part of your established drinking repertoire.

84

SANTAMANÍA

BRAND OWNER: Unique Spirits SL

DISTILLERY: Santamanía Urban Distillery, Las Rozas, Madrid, Spain

WEBSITE: www.santamania.com

VISITOR CENTRE: No

AVAILABILITY: Specialists

OTHER VARIANTS: Reserva (oak aged)

Here's something really quite unusual – a craft Spanish gin distillery, right in Madrid. Given the Spanish enthusiasm for gin, the skill and care with which it is served there and the massive range of brands you can find in almost any bar, you would assume that there are several small distilleries that have opened up to capitalise on this fantastic market, full of discriminating consumers.

Not so. In fact, as I write, this is Spain's only boutique gin distillery – think of it as a Sipsmith's and you'll begin to understand its importance. Santamanía in Spanish apparently suggests an obsessive attention to detail: well, the founders of this operation have certainly exhibited that.

To get started they had to argue over regulations and permissions for more than a year; they only ever make a maximum of 330 bottles at a time, but generally far fewer; they use grape spirit as their base and source unusual Spanish botanicals to give a distinctive twist to the final product.

The distilling process is a painstaking and labour-intensive one, involving twenty-four hours of maceration for the more robust botanicals, a full charge of their custom-built 280-litre Christian Carl still, use of a botanicals basket in a vapour chamber for the more delicate botanicals, a six-plate rectification column and then reduction with water brought specially from a Canary Islands volcano! After which the spirit rests for between two to three months before bottling. Every batch is individually identified and given a unique name and identity – these, maintain the distillers, are works of art.

Certainly the packaging stands apart, with a distinctive tall bottle with a funky red base that's covered in tiny etched detail – great fun to try to decode. First impressions on the nose are of red cherries, then liquorice root and a classic juniper bite. In total, fourteen botanicals are used, comprising juniper berries, coriander seed, liquorice root, fresh Spanish lime and lemon, angelica, orris root, Spanish pistachio nuts, raspberries, cinnamon, white pepper, dry ginger and rosemary. Quite a number of experimental batches were created before arriving at the final recipe, which, for such a young distillery, delivers an impressively mature and sophisticated product.

So, say 'hola!' to Santamanía, a Spanish gin that will shortly be popping up in great cocktail bars and collecting an impressive and well-deserved medal haul.

85

SHORTCROSS

BRAND OWNER:	Rademon Estate Distillery Ltd
DISTILLERY:	Rademon Estate Distillery, Downpatrick
WEBSITE:	www.shortcrossgin.com
VISITOR CENTRE:	No
AVAILABILITY:	Specialists
OTHER VARIANTS:	None

First impressions really count, and Shortcross have done exceptionally well here. Despite using a fairly dull standard bottle, the label is outstanding. The use of letterpress printing (I'm always a sucker for a nice piece of letterpress printing), the carefully selected typefaces and subtle use of foiling on the label, not to the mention the clever way the batch number is hidden on the reverse, means you can happily spend some time exploring the label before even thinking of opening the bottle. That may sound as if I need to get out more, but there's no denying the appeal of a satisfyingly tactile and well-designed piece of packaging. I was half sold on Shortcross before I tasted it; everything about the presentation told me that this gin had been made by people who cared, and naturally I expected that to be reflected in a quality product.

That's where the problem started. Shortcross have chosen to seal the bottle with a heavy black wax: it looks great, but took me as long to get off as I had spent savouring the label. These wax seals are the very devil to remove. You end up hacking at them with a knife, placing your fingers in considerable peril of being sliced off and generally end up with little bits of wax all over the place.

But it was worth it in the end. Though novice distillers, owners Fiona and David Boyd-Armstrong have gone to considerable pains to create something rather special for what is Northern Ireland's first boutique gin, and they've set the bar high. Apart from the lovely label (did I mention that?), the care and long planning is apparent in their choice of equipment.

Quite a number of small distillers use stills from Carl of Germany. Few have gone for a 450-litre copper pot still linked to two enrichment columns, each with seven individual bubble plates. It's a fine-looking piece of equipment that permits close control of the reflux during distillation, contributing to the delivery of a very smooth yet characterful spirit. With this particular design, Shortcross will have the flexibility to produce a number of alternative products, so expect further gin and doubtless a vodka before long.

The Boyd-Armstrongs wanted to create a gin that reflected its provenance, hence the foraged wild clover and homegrown green apples. There are elderflowers and elderberries also in the botanicals: the result is sweet but not cloying, with a satisfyingly spicy and herbal finish.

86

SIBLING

BRAND OWNER: Sibling Distillery Ltd

DISTILLERY: Sibling Distillery, Keynsham, Cheltenham

WEBSITE: www.siblingdistillery.com

VISITOR CENTRE: No, but you can visit Battledown Brewery

AVAILABILITY: Specialists

OTHER VARIANTS: None

Four fresh-faced and perfectly charming-looking young people look out at you earnestly from the Sibling website. It's not fair, but reading about the Elliot-Berry siblings – Felix (22), Clarice (20), Cicely (18) and Digby (15, yes, *15* – all at time of writing) – brought out my inner Victor Meldrew (not well hidden at the best of times).

With family connections to Cheltenham's Battledown Brewery, the group have certainly been exposed to the drinks trade from their earliest years. The family own Battledown, and logically this is the base for their operations. That knowledge of the drinks trade was the inspiration for them to found their own distillery, which, somewhat immodestly, they style 'ground-breaking' and 'the taste of a generation'. And, not lacking confidence, they went on to design their own still in the belief that it provides 'the platform to drive gin distilling forward'.

It is certainly different. The design is radical, featuring a stainless-steel pot and a twelve-foot-high glass column with integrated botanical baskets. Sibling first double-distil their own vodka, then run this spirit through the still once again with the botanicals suspended in the glass column, hence the description 'triple distilled'. Great play is made of the fact that they import vanilla directly from Madagascar and prepare blueberries by hand the day prior to distilling. The reduction water is apparently collected in the hills round Cheltenham, having been naturally filtered through a layer of fuller's earth (a bed of clay).

What we don't see in the still is any copper. It's very bold of Sibling to reject the very metal that, for hundreds of years, the rest of the distilling world has come to regard as essential. Bold, and probably a mistake, because for me this hasn't worked.

My impression – over sustained tasting and after soliciting other views – is that the nose is dominated by a stale note of overcooked vegetables (if it were whisky I would describe it as feinty, running to sulphury/vegetal), and the spirit is dull and lifeless on the palate. It finishes quite quickly, showing little complexity or evolution. This may simply be a problem with the sample I evaluated, and I sincerely hope so.

Notwithstanding these comments, I hope that Sibling succeeds. It's a lovely idea, but they may eventually find that overturning all conventional wisdom has set them apart rather more than they would have wished.

87

SILENT POOL

BRAND OWNER:	The Surrey Hills Distilling Company Ltd
DISTILLERY:	Silent Pool Distillery, Albury, Surrey
WEBSITE:	www.silentpooldistillers.com
VISITOR CENTRE:	Planned – check online for news
AVAILABILITY:	Specialists
OTHER VARIANTS:	None

By contrast with the youthful team we've just met at Sibling, Silent Pool can field some grizzled managers, including two highly qualified distillers, both MSc graduates of the renowned Heriot-Watt University distilling course, a commercially experienced veteran of the UK drinks distribution scene, and a couple of seasoned business executives with many years' experience who remain discreetly in the shadows while guiding the business's commercial destiny.

And despite being even newer than Sibling – in fact, they are one of the very newest operations mentioned here – it's clear that they know exactly what they are doing. An impressive Arnold Holstein copper pot still with a seven-plate rectifying column and 'gin head' has been installed and commissioned, allowing the distiller a huge variation in creating different spirits (future plans include whisky, vodka and liqueurs). Interestingly, the still itself is powered by steam from a wood-fired boiler.

The location, in a renovated barn on the Duke of Northumberland's Albury Estate is most attractive. The name comes from a local beauty spot, the Silent Pool, said to be sacred and linked to a thirteenth-century legend of a beautiful young woodcutter's daughter who would bathe in the pure, clear waters. One day a nobleman rode by and, overcome by her beauty, moved towards her (the beast!). But rather than give in to his advances, she waded deeper into the water and drowned. Her father recognised the man as King John. To this day locals claim that the girl can still be spotted at the Silent Pool at midnight, presumably somewhat bedraggled.

Well, I'm convinced. You won't catch me there, beautiful girl or not.

Silent Pool's new master distiller is Cory Mason, an American who has worked in top bars and craft distilling in the USA for more than fifteen years. As well as his Heriot-Watt MSc, Cory continues to work with the university, mentoring emerging distillers and conducting research for the spirits industry. He plans an innovative distilling regime and has sourced a number of interesting botanicals, including locally grown kaffir limes, pear and honey.

With strong industry credentials and attractive packaging, I expect Silent Pool to achieve rapid distribution in top cocktail bars – in fact, I shall be very surprised if it doesn't make quite a splash!

SIPSMITH

BRAND OWNER:	Sipsmith Ltd
DISTILLERY:	Sipsmith Distillery, Chiswick, London
WEBSITE:	www.sipsmith.com
VISITOR CENTRE:	Yes
AVAILABILITY:	Widespread
OTHER VARIANTS:	Very Juniper Over Proof (VJOP), Sloe

First there was Bombay, then Hendrick's, but if any one single brand can be said to have kick-started boutique craft gin distillation in the UK it is Sipsmith. Not, of course, that they intended to do that, but the wacky guys behind the well thought-out Sipsmith range have written the book on small-batch, hand-crafted, artisanal, authentic – all the adjectives, in fact, beloved of the new generation of distillers.

Their story begins in January 2007 when two old friends, Fairfax Hall and Sam Galsworthy quit their jobs, sold their respective houses and determined to create the distillery they'd been talking about for the last five years. Very soon, by a remarkable set of improbable coincidences, they found a suitable property (formerly used by the late, great Michael Jackson as a tasting room) that had once even been a micro-brewery. It then took two years of 'discussion' with HM Revenue and Customs to obtain a distilling licence.

Drinks writer Jared Brown then joined them as distiller and mastered the fine intricacies of Prudence, their original Christian Carl still. The bespoke design, combining a pot with a Carterhead and a column, makes for incredible versatility, allowing the distillation of both vodka and gin. The first production was in March 2009 and initial deliveries were made by hand, using Galsworthy's moped! Order after order followed, as gin took hold of the imagination of London's mixologists and their customers; less than a year later major supermarkets and off-licences were stocking the brand. Very soon afterwards a second still, Patience, was installed.

Several other expressions, including the mighty VJOP, have followed and, more recently, a move to enlarged premises in Chiswick with further distillation capacity in the form of Constance, their third still. The new distillery will also eventually feature a micro-distilling set-up for product development. The partners, all still active in the business, are rightly proud of what has been achieved, and there are regular 'pop-up' events at the distillery.

Sipsmith have achieved incredible growth in a very short time and become something of a poster boy for the craft distilling movement, inspiring others to follow in their footsteps. Few will be quite as successful, but if they have half the fun and make gin half as good their life will be an exciting and rewarding one.

89

SIX O'CLOCK

BRAND OWNER: Bramley & Gage

DISTILLERY: Bramley & Gage, Thornbury, Bristol

WEBSITE: www.bramleyandgage.co.uk

VISITOR CENTRE: Distillery tours available

AVAILABILITY: Limited

OTHER VARIANTS: Sloe, organic sloe and damson

I say, chaps, here's a good idea: a gin with its own tonic. And what better name for an English gin than 'Six O'Clock'? After all, as any serious gin drinker knows, it's always six o'clock somewhere and that's all the excuse you need to break out the tonic and ice.

But there's a wonderful story here. Bramley & Gage were originally fruit farmers in South Devon but, one day, realised that strawberries were a great deal more valuable as a fruit liqueur than as fresh fruit. So they started making fruit liqueurs and pretty soon sold the farm and concentrated on this full time.

A new generation of the family took over running the business in 2007. They took their first footsteps into gin and, in May 2013, raised £24,000 to buy a still with support from 248 backers on Funding Circle, a crowd-funding website. They worked hard to sell Six O'Clock Gin and were very soon able to buy a brand new Rolls-Royce for all their employees and take three months off every year at their estate in the Caribbean (I may have imagined the last part, from 'brand new Rolls-Royce'). But it has been a success and a well-deserved one, with national listings in at least one major supermarket and a gold medal or two.

It's an absolutely straight-down-the-road classic English gin, juniper to the fore but elegant, well mannered and quite deliciously refreshing. The website and label has a lot of nonsense about the 'ginspiration' coming from the current MD's great-grandfather, claiming that his 'balance, poise and precision' contributed to their selection of botanicals. I don't believe a word of it! If this were my creation I'd trumpet the fact, and highlight the jolly good value that Six O'Clock offers if you're looking for something a little out of the ordinary.

For all that, it's quite a simple recipe, using just seven botanicals, including orange peel and elderflower. That's a component that I feel, used sensitively, works very well to add both freshness and sweetness. With Six O'Clock's own tonic (such a clever idea that I'm surprised more distillers don't follow suit), it's a clean, light and zesty little sharpener that I'm sure you could be excused for trying at lunchtime. Just the one, mind.

Bramley & Gage also make various flavoured gins under their own B&G banner, such as sloe, organic sloe and damson gin, and it's possible to arrange a tour of the distillery to see for yourself.

90

SLOANE'S

BRAND OWNER:	Toorank Distilleries BV, Zevenaar, The Netherlands
DISTILLERY:	Toorank, Zevenaar, The Netherlands
WEBSITE:	www.sloanes-gin.com
VISITOR CENTRE:	No
AVAILABILITY:	Limited
OTHER VARIANTS:	None

Sloane's: you would imagine, wouldn't you, that the name is a reference to the Sloane Ranger, the archetypal upper-class Londoner whose self-possessed, braying tones one could quite convincingly imagine ordering a large G&T with all the confidence and privilege associated with the label (if you're reading this in the USA, think 'preppy'). But you'd be wrong.

The serious-minded Dutch distillers had another Londoner in mind: inspired by Sir Hans Sloane's (1660–1753) personal botanical collection which formed the foundation of the British and Natural History Museum collections.

We can't of course be sure – and (being a gentleman) Sloane does not appear to have any documented connection to the gin trade, but it is suggested by Toorank that Sloane's botanicals introduced to the UK a number of then exotic ingredients such as juniper berries, fresh oranges and lemons, orris root, angelica, cardamom, coriander, cassia bark, liquorice and vanilla. These, of course, have formed the basis for creating gins ever since. It's a pleasing theory, even if the historical evidence may be lacking. After all, London's Worshipful Company of Distillers was founded more than twenty years before Sloane was born and published *The Distiller of London,* a book of rules and instructions, as early as 1638.

Toorank are actually a large contract distiller, producing third-party products, as well as their own brands. They set some bold objectives for Sloane's and have gone about distilling it in a particularly meticulous way. Using a relatively small still, each of the ten botanicals is distilled separately, left to rest for between two to three months before being blended together and then rested again, prior to bottling. They use only fresh fruit, rather than peel, evident in the marked citrus note and clean fresh nose.

Shortly after it launched, Sloane's was awarded World's Best Gin and Best White Spirit, and was a Double Gold Medal winner at the San Francisco World Spirit Competition in 2011. As far as I can determine, it hasn't been placed at any major awards subsequently, but the company may have decided to rest on their laurels for a while as this led to an unexpected and hard-to-manage surge in demand.

It's well worth tracking down – just try to ask for it nicely, yah.

91

SPRING 44

BRAND OWNER: Spring 44 Distilling Inc.

DISTILLERY: Spring 44, Loveland, Colorado, USA

WEBSITE: www.spring44.com

VISITOR CENTRE: Distillery tours available

AVAILABILITY: USA only at present

OTHER VARIANTS: Old Tom, Mountain

This remote Colorado distillery – well, remote if you live in London or somewhere, and this is one of the USA's less populous states, anyway– is getting a lot of attention right now from better bars over there. Or, to put it another way, pretty soon we're going to be seeing it over here, assuming for a moment that they can make enough to satisfy demand; always a problem for a smaller distiller once the market decides that something is hot.

While the distillery itself is located in the town of Loveland, the water source sounds absolutely fabulous. Right in the northern Rocky Mountains it lies on a property purchased by the Lindauer family in 1969, which is accessible only by navigating an eleven-mile dirt road, culminating with a 2½-mile jeep trail involving a climb of some 2,000 feet into the Buckthorn Canyon. There aren't many neighbours: only 160,000 acres of National Forest. But I'd like to think there are wolves and grizzlies, though that may be my imagination running away with me.

That natural spring, source of Spring 44's artesian water, became the foundation for creating their craft spirits. Visiting the spring to drink directly from it had become something of a family ritual, and in autumn 2008 Jeff Lindauer and his friend Russ Wall (who is now in charge of their marketing) were doing just that when the idea of a distillery took hold. They were joined by more friends and so the company was born.

Their timing was good, with interest growing in products that could claim quality, sustainability, authenticity and transparency, and the craft distilling movement gaining credibility and momentum, especially in the USA. Their story resonated with consumers, and their fame spread to the point where, as I say, Spring 44 gin is being tipped as the coming thing.

The rather handsome bottle features a juniper berry on the label and, though they don't provide details of their twelve botanicals, the juniper note is distinctly pronounced. The spirit base is their own multi-grain blend of wheat, rye and corn, filtered through a coconut husk filtration system (though to be completely honest I have no idea why this should make the slightest difference).

Their tasting room is open on Saturdays (tours can be booked online), but, better still, they have their own happy hour: the distillery is open to the public for cocktails and fun every Friday from 4 p.m. to 7 p.m. Other distillers, please note!

92

ST GEORGE'S TERROIR

BRAND OWNER: St George's Spirits

DISTILLERY: St George's Spirits, Alameda, California, USA

WEBSITE: www.stgeorgespirits.com

VISITOR CENTRE: Distillery tours available

AVAILABILITY: Limited

OTHER VARIANTS: Botanivore, Dry Rye Gin

Wow! Just, wow! The first time I tasted this it absolutely took my breath away, such is the unexpected nature of the taste and the explosive impact of the first sip. And it was just as remarkable on the second and subsequent occasions. In fact, I think I can say that out of all the gins that I tasted for this book this was the one that lingered longest and I could recall most distinctly the next day.

That's not always a good thing, however. I can think of one or two that were memorable for all the wrong reasons (they didn't make the cut, needless to say), but, while this is a love-it-or-hate-it kind of a spirit, it's clearly made with a point of view. Or perhaps attitude would be more apt, for this hails from the St George's Spirits distillery in Alameda, California, arguably the birthplace of the modern American artisan distillation movement. This was founded in 1982 by Jörg Rupf, a German immigrant with family connections to the distilling of fruit spirits in the Black Forest. He established a small distillery to recreate the products he remembered from Germany and, in the process, changed everything that was then known about distilling in the USA.

Several other very well-known artisan distillers in the USA trained here and have gone on to establish their own operations, often with considerable success. And St George's, now owned by Lance Winters, has grown to the point where it now occupies a 65,000-square-feet building and operates a number of stills, making a full range of spirits.

They describe the *terroir* as 'inspired by the forests of Northern California' and suggest that 'the taste will transport you somewhere beautiful and wild'. Included in the botanicals are Douglas fir, California bay laurel and coastal sage along with nine other more conventional botanicals. They distil the fir and sage individually on a 250-litre still to minimise the impact of seasonal variation, while the fresh bay laurel leaves and juniper berries are vapour infused in a botanicals basket and the other botanicals go right into their 1,500-litre pot still. The result is a walk in the pinewoods.

It's remarkable. Whether this can truly be called gin is debatable. I doubt most gin drinkers would find it acceptable but I will admit that I went back to the glass time after time, if only to confirm that I hadn't imagined its dramatic, intense aromas and taste. In fact, I'm pining for it now.

STRANE MERCHANT STRENGTH

BRAND OWNER: Smögen Whisky AB

DISTILLERY: Smögen Whisky AB,
Hunnebostrand, Sweden

WEBSITE: www.strane.se

VISITOR CENTRE: Distillery tours available by
appointment

AVAILABILITY: Specialists

OTHER VARIANTS: Navy Strength, Uncut

Gin? From a whisky distillery? In Sweden? Yes, it's all true. Smögen Whisky was established in 2010 by lawyer and whisky author turned distiller Pär Caldenby and has proved one of the success stories of Swedish craft distilling (there have been failures).

They make three gins, all in small quantities, in a tiny 100-litre wood-fired pot still. True to their whisky roots, blending is at the heart of what they do, and the production process at Strane is both interesting and unusual. Actually, Hendrick's does something similar and, curious but true, that's also made by a company better known for its whisky.

Beginning with the same twelve botanicals (juniper, coriander, sage, lime and lemon peel, basil, mint, sweet almond, cinnamon, liquorice and two secret ingredients native to Sweden) Caldenby uses them to create three separate distillates with distinct flavours. The separate distillates – not finished gins at this stage – one junipery, the second citrus dominated and the third more herbal are then blended in different ratios to create three final products. Simples! Whisky blenders do this all the time, except they use the products of different distilleries and varying cask types.

The thinking behind this is to emphasise and consistently deliver the flavour of each group of botanicals, exploiting the fact that different botanicals behave differently at different boiling points. Rather than adopting a 'one size fits all' approach, this allows the team scope to explore the subtler notes in each.

The base spirits are then blended to produce the three expressions, Merchant, Navy and Uncut – all are bottled at different strengths and quite distinctive in style and flavour. Of course the key to product consistency then lies in the blending, exactly like a blended Scotch whisky. The first and most widely available is their Merchant Strength, itself a chunky 47.4% bruiser; the Uncut reaches an alarming 75.3% abv – it's not for the unwary!

Gin made like this, at a higher strength, in small batches, in a high-wage economy such as Sweden's is never going to be cheap. You'll find Strane in a few UK specialists at around £40 for their 50cl bottle (the equivalent of £56 for a standard bottle), which pushes it into super-premium territory. So it's probably more of a special treat than an everyday tipple, unless those secret Swedish botanicals really float your boat.

94

TANQUERAY TEN

BRAND OWNER: Diageo plc

DISTILLERY: Cameronbridge, Fife

WEBSITE: www.tanqueray.com

VISITOR CENTRE: No

AVAILABILITY: Widespread

OTHER VARIANTS: Tanqueray Export Strength, Rangpur, Malacca and Old Tom (limited editions)

Here's proof – if proof were needed – that big brands can be cool, sexy and very, very good. Because this super-premium expression of one of the USA's favourite gins is all those things: it's what's in the bottle that counts, and here we have a gin that any distiller would be proud to offer up, any fashionable cocktail watering hole happy to mix and any discerning drinker more than content to savour.

Tanqueray started life in London in 1830 but has had an itinerant existence since the Second World War. It now seems settled in its own dedicated gin hall located within Diageo's giant Cameronbridge distilling complex – unfortunately, so large and busy is the site it seems unlikely that public access will ever be possible. Never mind: I popped in to take a look for you and I can report it is both hugely impressive and reassuringly calm.

Under the watchful eye of master distiller Tom Nichol, the venerable 'Old Tom No. 4a' still and its diminutive fellow 'Tiny Tim' both seem well settled in their Scottish home. Both are vital to Tanqueray Ten: the citrus heart of the spirit is first distilled in Tiny Tim using fresh chopped oranges, limes and grapefruit, and this is then transferred to the larger, hand-riveted Old Tom, where juniper (more than in the standard version), coriander, angelica, liquorice, chamomile flowers and more limes are added.

In order to preserve the vibrant citrus character, only 60% of the final run is selected to go forward for reduction and eventual bottling. Unusually, Tanqueray is made using the 'one shot' process, another nod to tradition and further evidence of the carefully crafted nature of this superb creation. Finally, I'm glad to say that it's reassuringly strong (something to remember when comparing prices). At 47.3% this offers body, mouthfeel and a delightfully mouth-coating creaminess; this is a classic that continues to deliver from aroma to finish.

Indeed, I'd go so far as to say that you might never need to try another gin ever again. But in doing that you would deny yourself the considerable pleasure of Tanqueray's limited edition releases Malacca and Old Tom, which, though they were only produced for a short run, may still be found on some bar and specialist shelves.

I don't do marks, but I give Ten 10/10.

95

TANQUERAY RANGPUR

BRAND OWNER:	Diageo plc
DISTILLERY:	Cameronbridge, Fife
WEBSITE:	www.tanqueray.com
VISITOR CENTRE:	No
AVAILABILITY:	Widespread
OTHER VARIANTS:	Tanqueray Export Strength, Ten, Malacca and Old Tom (limited editions)

I hope you're not worried this is out of the otherwise impeccably organised alphabetical order that characterises the rest of this book. Strictly speaking, it should appear before Tanqueray Ten but there is a sound reason I haven't put it there.

I'm channelling my inner Coleridge who famously wrote to his friend and poet Robert Southey, railing against the dull conformity of strict alphabetical ordering, describing it as 'an arrangement determined by the accident of initial letters'. Actually, that's not really the reason, but it's always amusing to see if one can work in some not entirely spurious reference to the Lake Poets. Coleridge makes a brief if unsavoury appearance in gin's history in Wordsworth's 1812 description of him as 'a rotten drunkard, rotting out his entrails by intemperance and in the habit of running into debt at little Pot-houses for Gin' – a reminder of gin's darker days and generally sleazy reputation just a few years before Charles Tanqueray opened the doors of his distillery in London's Bloomsbury.

Anyway, these two are in this order because Ten is the more classical in style of the two, and Rangpur something of an outlier in terms of flavour. However, being a sucker for more citrus-led flavours I'm going to come right out and say that I love this, even if it must have come as a shock to regular Tanqueray drinkers.

So what's it all about? First launched in the USA in 2006 it adds ginger, bay leaves and – as you've worked out from the name – Rangpur limes to the usual botanicals. Being honest, I'll admit I had to look those up, whereupon I learned that Rangpur limes apparently have the juiciness of an orange and the zestiness of a lime. What a versatile little fruit it is, also it seems, known as Canton lemon in South China, hime lemon in Japan, cravo lemon in Brazil, and mandarin lime in the United States. It's a hybrid between the mandarin orange and the lemon. I think that's probably enough: I'm starting to show off.

The point is the big citrus flavour. The good old Rangpur lime has put on its size twelve boots and marched all over this. Some hard-core gin aficionados don't care for it over much. Simon Difford compares it to a Tanqueray Gimlet. What's wrong with that, I ask. Sounds great!

It's bold, experimental, innovative and quite funky: all the things big brands are supposed not to be.

96

TARQUIN'S

BRAND OWNER: Southwestern Distillery Ltd

DISTILLERY: Southwestern Distillery, St Ervan, Wadebridge, Cornwall

WEBSITE: www.southwesterndistillery.com

VISITOR CENTRE: Possibly in 2016. Contact distillery for details.

AVAILABILITY: Specialists

OTHER VARIANTS: None

$\mathcal{S}_o$ where did we leave Tanqueray? Ah yes, I'd just described Rangpur as 'bold, experimental, innovative and quite funky: all the things big brands are supposed not to be', and here we are with Tarquin Leadbetter of the eponymous Tarquin's gin which one could describe as bold, experimental, innovative and quite funky. All the things a small craft distiller is supposed to be in fact.

I was interested to read his blog for 24 January 2013 when he had just got started. He began: 'It has been 220,240 hours since my last paid employment (in a bar), and over 400,000 hours since I last worked behind a desk. In this period, I had over 4,988 sips of gin and pastis, tasting about 100 different brands. I sent and received 8,132 emails, drove 11,001 miles (had one puncture) and grew a beard for 90.6 days, a personal record.' It might be worth rereading that if you were thinking of starting your own distillery. In fact, you might want to print it out and stick it where you (and your partner) can gaze thoughtfully upon it on a regular basis. Without labouring the point, starting your own business is seriously hard work and, fun though it may seem, starting a distillery is no different. (Writing, on the other hand, is a breeze. The world definitely needs more writers and drinks books in particular are in short supply. Note use of irony here.)

Tarquin's is batch distilled in Tarquin's direct-fired copper pot still (a very similar set-up to that at 58 Gin) and, using the one shot method, he is able to produce a maximum of 300 bottles. Interestingly, Tanqueray also adopts this approach though they make rather more. Their distiller doesn't then bottle and wax seal each bottle.

He has picked some unusual but not completely outrageous botanicals, including fresh citrus fruits, cacao, pink peppercorns and violet leaves. With great local support Tarquin's have now reached the point where they have been able to install a second still and, at the time of writing, are looking to employ a brand ambassador to sell in London. It just proves what can be done – but by now the hours, miles and emails will have grown quite extensively.

Good luck to him. Anyone who can also distil the UK's first aniseed spirit and call it Cornish Pastis deserves to succeed!

97

TWO BIRDS

BRAND OWNER: Union Distillers Ltd

DISTILLERY: Union Distillery, Market Harborough, Leicestershire

WEBSITE: www.twobirdsspirits.co.uk

VISITOR CENTRE: Yes

AVAILABILITY: Specialists

OTHER VARIANTS: Cocktail Strength (trade only), Sipping Gin, Hogarth's Old Tom

Right out of its nest, Two Birds was awarded Gold Medal (UK Craft Gin of the Year) at the Craft Gin Awards 2013. Not bad for this fledgling firm of distillers, based in Market Harborough and producing their spirits on a still of their own design.

Co-owner Mark Gamble is himself an electrical engineer, so he designed and built their twenty-five-litre copper and brass still himself, nicknaming it 'Gerard's No. 1'. I have no idea who Gerard might be, and while it's more usual to give a gin still a lady's name, there's no law against making it masculine if that's what takes your fancy. By the way, this really and truly is a small-batch operation: Gerard can only make around one hundred bottles per four-hour distillation run, so volumes are always going to be very limited.

The botanicals in Two Birds are really held to the minimum; there being a mere five components. What they are remains a strict trade secret, but apart from the key ingredient of juniper (it's fairly obvious the moment you nose this) and what I suspect is orris root (for smoothness and to integrate the gin), I believe there is a citrus element playing its part. What this does show is that it's perfectly possible, indeed you might argue even desirable, to make a perfectly decent gin in the classic London Dry style without complicating matters with a very long list of increasingly arcane ingredients.

However, if the product is simple in its construction don't be fooled. This will stand comparison with any number of the bigger brands and represents a very drinkable, mainstream gin that will work well in a G&T and a range of cocktails. For the drinks trade Two Birds have cleverly devised a more assertive juniper-influenced version, Cocktail Gin – the name should let you work out what it's designed to do.

Alongside the straightforward recipe goes straightforward but nonetheless charming packaging. Our old friend the Oslo bottle, apparently the default choice of the craft distilling industry, makes another appearance here, this time dressed in simple hand-drawn graphics that reflect the gin's 'countryside spirit'.

I'd love to see this at a higher strength, say 46% abv, which I feel would add just a little bit of punch and weight to what is a very agreeable, well-made and straightforward gin and let those Two Birds soar even higher! But perhaps that's over-egging it (sorry, didn't even try to resist that).

UNGAVA

BRAND OWNER:	Domaine Pinnacle Inc., Frelighsburg, Quebec, Canada
DISTILLERY:	Domaine Pinnacle, Cowansville, Quebec, Canada
WEBSITE:	www.ungava-gin.com
VISITOR CENTRE:	Boutique available to visit (though primarily for cider)
AVAILABILITY:	Specialists
OTHER VARIANTS:	None

We haven't had a gin from Canada yet, so this piqued my curiosity. The name and packaging are funky and the colour draws the eye. Ah yes, that colour. When the company's president told Canada's *MacLean's Magazine* that it was 'a bit like morning's vitamin-enriched urine', there's not a lot more to say. Let's move on.

Ungava comes from Quebec and contains some seriously obscure botanicals in an effort to create a gin that is truly, pre-colonially Canadian. So, some forty indigenous herbs, berries and flowers (anything planted by Europeans was out) finally gave way to just six ingredients, all found on the Ungava Peninsula in Nunavik: cloudberries, crowberries, Labrador tea, Ukiurtatuq, or 'Arctic blend' (basically another plant used by native people to make tea), and of course juniper, without which Ungava wouldn't be proper gin (ha, so they do pay some attention to us Europeans, after all). And the crazy colour: that comes from the sixth ingredient, wild rosehips.

The company themselves get pretty lyrical about Ungava, a vast and wild territory at the northern edge of Quebec. Its Inuit meaning is 'towards the open water' and it's described as 'a place of indescribable beauty whose splendour is heightened by the celestial light show of the aurora borealis and the immensity of its landscapes' et cetera et cetera. Their publicity goes on in this vein at some length – not so indescribable after all, it turns out. But, as I haven't been there and won't be going any time soon, we'll take their word for it.

Once a year, two hardy Inuit chaps from Kuujjuag head out to pick the botanicals. They've got just four weeks to harvest several hundred kilos which are then sent about 900 miles south to a micro-distillery in Cowansville, about an hour's drive from Montreal. A neutral spirit made with locally grown corn is infused with the botanicals. From start to finish, it takes about a month to make a batch of gin, which comes out of the distillery at 72% alcohol and then gets diluted to 43.1% for bottling. Along the way, the Nunavik botanicals are added at the beginning of the process, and again towards the end.

Maintaining the Inuit connection, the funny squiggles on the label aren't some meaningless jumble of lines, but Inuktitut. I haven't the slightest idea what it means. Sorry.

99

WARNER EDWARDS
HARRINGTON DRY

BRAND OWNER: Warner Edwards Distillery Ltd

DISTILLERY: Warner Edwards, Hall Farm, Harrington, North Hampshire

WEBSITE: www.warneredwards.com

VISITOR CENTRE: Yes

AVAILABILITY: Limited

OTHER VARIANTS: Elderflower, Sloe and Rhubarb styles

I hesitate to refer to anyone as 'passionate' about their product. The problem with this perfectly good, inoffensive and hitherto useful word is that it has been entirely devalued by the marketing community (PR folks are particularly egregious offenders). 'Passion' is everywhere, and as a result it's nowhere, empty of all meaning; a cliché that has been hollowed out and now lies dully on the page, gasping for its last breath like a stranded dolphin.

Unfortunately I can't think of another word to describe Tom Warner's enthusiasm for his product. Talking to him, it was hard to get a word in edgeways; such was the tumbling rush of ardent advocacy that I was quite caught up in his zeal. Here, I felt, was a man alive with a mission to share, to explain, to proselytise about his product so intensely that I may as well have been in the presence of the Ancient Mariner – not the gin, you can read about that on another page – and I could not choose but listen.

And what a great story he tells. Warner Edwards Harrington Dry has been created by two chums from agricultural college (Tom and business partner Sion Edwards) looking for an escape from a life of corporate conformity by embracing the vicissitudes of self-employment; something, incidentally, which I can entirely empathise with, having long since fallen foul of dull convention. And several employers.

Springing as they both do from long-established farming stock they looked first at distilling essential oils from lavender they planned to grow on the family farms. They briefly toyed with making vodka but, thankfully, then remembered they liked gin. Hallelujah!

Being committed to the idea, they bought one of the first small Holstein stills in the UK and fired it up in December 2012 (that's a measure of just how new this craft gin phenomenon is) and have gone from strength to strength.

And so they should. This is a bold and proudly assertive, juniper-led, peppery and complex product that should appeal to traditionalists looking to push the boundaries of flavour just a little, without anything too outrageous or provocatively unconventional. Use in cocktails where you want the gin to shine through, and for best results in a G&T, don't overdo the tonic. Judges at the San Francisco World Spirits Competition thought highly enough of this to award it Double Gold – one each for Tom and Sion, presumably, united in spirit.

100

WHITLEY NEILL

BRAND OWNER: Halewood International
Holdings plc

DISTILLERY: The Langley Distillery, Langley
Green, Warley, West Midlands

WEBSITE: www.whitleyneill.com

VISITOR CENTRE: No

AVAILABILITY: Limited

OTHER VARIANTS: None

Drat! More of that pesky dark glass that doesn't allow you to see how much is left in the bottle. Aren't those bottles annoying? Gin is a wonderfully clear and bright spirit, so why hide it away? Anyway, enough of that bugbear: we're approaching the end of this wonderful gin odyssey and that's reason enough to be cheerful.

What we have here is another gin inspired by Africa (I trust you've remembered the elephants) but brought to us by Johnny Neill, fourth generation member of the Greenall Whitley distilling dynasty. He's got gin in his blood and, as it happens, a South African wife. Taking that as his cue, he turned to the physalis plant and the baobab tree, known as the 'tree of life', to add the flavour of the Dark Continent to this most English of spirits. Its strange, otherworldly, upside-down form features as the brand's logo, though the website features a most striking African lady on the welcome page, just in case you hadn't got the message.

Launched in 2007, Whitley Neill was an early entrant into the small-batch gin scene and has since picked up a hatful of medals for its complex, spicy taste with the layered earth notes, hints of tropical fruits and lemons and peppery finish. Much play is made on their website of the copper pot still (Constance, since you asked) used to make the gin, and which is said to be England's oldest. I don't actually think this matters, though you may feel it adds a certain corroborative and romantic detail to the story.

Perhaps surprisingly, there is only one product: no flavoured variant, no navy strength, not even some 'limited edition' expression. There is of course some merit in single-minded consistency if building a brand and, as Johnny Neill claims to have learned about gin at his grandmother's knee (and other low joints I don't doubt), long-term thinking probably runs in the family. In a market driven by experimentation and more than a degree of short-lived fashionability it will be interesting to see how this approach serves the brand.

I think that's probably about it. Time that you put this down and picked up a refreshing G&T, White Lady, Negroni, Old Etonian or Martini. I told you that gin was simply The Last Word. And, with that, I'm off for a handy Corpse Reviver No. 2. Pip! Pip!

No. Wait. There's one more. And trust me, gin number 101 is an absolute cracker!

101

XORIGUER

BRAND OWNER: Pons family

DISTILLERY: Destilerias Xoriguer, Mahón, Menorca

WEBSITE: www.xoriguer.co.uk

VISITOR CENTRE: No

AVAILABILITY: Limited

OTHER VARIANTS: None

Having begun with a numeral and then gone straight into the letter 'A', I was determined that I would finish this book with a 'Z'. I decided that Zuidam didn't count because that's the name of the distillery (their gin is Dutch Courage). But there is a Zebra gin apparently, distilled by the splendidly named Four Stars Beverages Ltd of Plot 183/189 Bombo Road Kawempe-Kazo, Kampala, in Uganda. But my joy was short lived – could I find a bottle? What do you think? Those stripes are better camouflage than you first realise.

So we must conclude with Xoriguer from the Spanish Balearic island of Menorca (which, though most of it is drunk there, you will be able to find) and which turns out to have the most fascinating story imaginable. For one thing, now that Plymouth has given up its protected origin status there are only two gins left in the world enjoying recognition as a local speciality (the other is Vilnius from Lithuania). And, like Plymouth, there's a connection to the Jolly Jack Tars of Britain's Royal Navy. In the eighteenth century Menorca was British and we had a huge base there. And, in the middle of the gin craze, what do you imagine thirsty British matelots wanted to drink? Hint: the answer is not 'rum'. So the locals made gin for them, and today they're still at it.

And, unusually, it is distilled using a base of Mediterranean wine alcohol but comes off the wood-fired stills at its 38% bottling strength. It comes in a seriously funky bottle with a label that is genuinely retro, largely because no one has got round to changing it in years. What's not to like?

It gets better. It is, of course, still family-owned and distilled to a secret recipe. Apparently only heirs of the founder Miguel Pons Justo are permitted to receive the super-classified details and proportions of the vital ingredients, and, before they add them to the still, the doors are locked and any witnesses killed. Actually, I made that last bit up – they just politely ask them to leave. But say you did believe me, if only for a moment.

Before bottling it is rested in oak. You can find a bottle here in the UK for around £22. I can't tell you how happy it has made me to track down Xoriguer (say it sho-ri-gair): a truly artisanal gin, with deep and long-standing connections to the great days of English gin distilling that is still alive and flourishing as we enter a new gin craze.

Bottoms up, ladies and gentlemen!

ACKNOWLEDGEMENTS

Thanks are due to all the distillers, too many to mention by name, who let me look around their distilleries and patiently answered my tedious and no doubt naïve questions. My wife Lindsay patiently put up with the vicissitudes of my moods while writing this book (but I suspect the sampling helped); my agent Judy Moir skilfully guided me through the arcane rituals of actually getting a publisher interested; and the team at said publisher, Birlinn – especially Neville Moir, Alison Rae, Anna Marshall and Jan Rutherford (dedicated gin drinkers all) – were committed and enthusiastic supporters.

The gin industry generously stepped up with samples and to all the 101 listed here and to the others who responded but I have disappointed, my thanks. And, to the few who spurned my entreaties, I trust you're feeling good about that right now. Special thanks to Andrew Auwerda (Philadelphia Distilling); Alex Nicol (Spencerfield Spirits) and Master of Malt's Ben Ellefsen and his colleagues who helped get this off the ground.

All trademarks are acknowledged, and all product images are the copyright property of the relevant brand owner, reproduced with permission.

OTHER RESOURCES AND FURTHER READING

THE WEB

There is, inevitably, a host of websites, blogs and other resources to be found online. Virtually all the brands maintain a website and a presence on social media, and some even manage to keep up a blog with reasonable frequency. Brand websites are listed in the individual entries.

Some independent blogs that I have found of consistent value are:

www.ginfoundry.com – the organisers of the rather wonderful Junipalooza Festival, where I first met many of the producers listed here, run this excellent site which is constantly updated with news and views on the world of gin.

www.diffordsguide.com – Simon Difford who literally wrote the book on gin (see below) maintains this invaluable site, with a host of reviews on all varieties of beer, wines and spirits. It's where the trade go for information.

www.gintime.com – *Classic Gin* by Geraldine Coates is sadly out of print now, but this Edinburgh-based author has brought her considerable expertise and many years of authority to this site.

www.theginisin.com – established in 2009, this US-based site claims to be 'the original gin blog'. A great place for reviews with well over 200 and counting.

www.juniperdiaries.co.uk – a lively UK enthusiast site, with very open reviews.

Given the importance of gin in Spain, there are a number of Spanish-language blogs that appear interesting, but as I don't speak Spanish it's hard to recommend any!

BOOKS

I found the following to be useful.

Gin. The Much-Lamented Death of Madam Geneva, Patrick Dillon (Headline, 2002). A wonderfully absorbing and fast-moving account of the original Gin Craze. Considerable archive research is apparent, but this reads almost like a thriller.

Craze, Jessica Warner (Profile Books, 2003). A surprisingly lively account of the eighteenth-century Gin Craze in London and a provocative discussion of the lessons for today's 'War on Drugs'.

The Spirit of Gin, Matt Teacher (Cider Mill Press, 2014). Rather US-centric but great to dip into for good information on production, history and cocktails.

Difford's Gin Compendium, Simon Difford (Old Firm of Sin, 2013). A beautifully produced and thoughtful compilation with detailed profiles of eighteen leading distillers and a lengthy brand listing with tasting notes and ratings.

Gin Annual (2014) (Gin Foundry, 2014). A review of the year, with brand features and commentary. Presumably intended to be an annual publication, I anticipate this to build into a valuable, long-term resource.

A number of brands, most notable Beefeater, Bombay, Greenall's and Plymouth have produced their own corporate histories. While fascinating, it should be recalled that they are not entirely disinterested and will see the world through the eyes of their own brand.

COCKTAILS

Cocktails are hugely important to gin – or rather gin is hugely important to cocktails – so naturally there is a significant body of literature on the subject. In recent years a number of authors have revisited the classics and developed exciting new cocktails. There is, of course, a huge amount to be found on the web, but there is no substitute for a handsome book.

The Savoy Cocktail Book, Harry Craddock. First published in 1930 and still in print, this is probably the best starting point for any education in cocktails.

Cocktails: The Bartender's Bible, Simon Difford (Firefly Books, 2013). Three thousand recipes from a modern spirits guru.

The Drunken Botanist, Amy Stewart (Timber Press, 2013). A look at the science underpinning key botanical ingredients.

Other names to look out for include Tony Conigliaro, Dale DeGroff, Gary Regan, Tristan Stephenson and Dave Wondrich. The world of cocktails has a rich and absorbing literature before you even mix a drink.